CASE STUDIES IN
EDUCATION AND CULTURE

General Editors

GEORGE *and* LOUISE SPINDLER
Stanford University

T

A BORNEO CHILDHOOD
Enculturation in Dusun Society

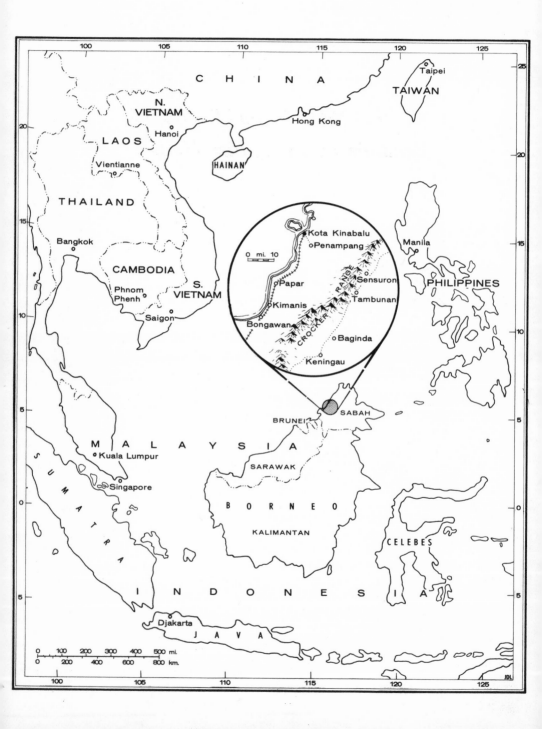

A BORNEO CHILDHOOD

Enculturation in Dusun Society

THOMAS RHYS WILLIAMS
The Ohio State University

HOLT, RINEHART AND WINSTON
New York • Chicago • San Francisco • Atlanta
Dallas • Montreal • Toronto • London • Sydney

Copyright © 1969 by Holt, Rinehart and Winston, Inc.
Library of Congress Catalog Card Number: 73-94351
SBN: 03-082822-8
Printed in the United States of America
1 2 3 4 5 6 7 8 9

Foreword

/

About the Series

This series of case studies in education and culture is designed to bring to students in professional education and in the social sciences the results of direct observation and participation in the educational process in a variety of cultural settings. Individual studies include some devoted to single classrooms, others focus on single schools, some on large communities and their schools; still others report on indigenous cultural transmission where there are no schools at all in the Western sense. Every attempt is made to move beyond the formalistic treatments of educational process to the interaction between the people engaged in educative events, their thinking and feeling, and the content of the educational process in which they are engaged. Each study is basically descriptive in character but since all of them are about education they are also problem oriented. Interpretive generalizations are produced inductively. Some are stated explicitly by the authors of the studies. Others are generated in the reader's mind as hypotheses about education and its environmental relationships.

The cross-cultural emphasis of the series is particularly significant. Education is a cultural process. Each new member of a society or a group must learn to act appropriately as a member and contribute to its maintenance and, occasionally, to its improvement. Education, in every cultural setting, is an instrument for survival. It is also an instrument for adaptation and change. To understand education we must study it as it is—imbedded in the culture of which it is an integral part and which it serves.

When education is studied this way, the generalizations about the relationship between schools and communities, educational and social systems, education and cultural setting that are current in modern educational discussions become meaningful. This series is, therefore, intended for use in courses in comparative and overseas education, social foundations and the sociology of education, international educational development, culture and personality, social psychology, cultural dynamics and cultural transmission, comparative sociology—wherever the interdependency of education and culture, and education and society, is particularly relevant.

We hope these studies will be useful as resources for comparative analyses, and for stimulating thinking and discussion about education that is not confined by one's own cultural experience. Without this exercise of a comparative, transcultural perspective it seems unlikely that we can acquire a clear view of our own educational experience or view education in other cultural settings without ethnocentric bias.

About the Author

Thomas Rhys Williams is a professor and chairman of the Department of Anthropology at The Ohio State University. He holds a Master of Arts degree from the University of Arizona and a doctoral degree from Syracuse University. He has engaged in field research among the Papago of Arizona and the native peoples of Borneo. His interests in field research include enculturation, social structure, nonverbal communication, and cultural structuring of perceptions. He has published several professional articles, a case study, and a methods study of the Dusun of Sabah and is completing a text on the topic of socialization. He is a Fellow of the American Anthropological Association and a member of the Society of Sigma Xi and other professional associations.

About the Book

This case study, unlike the others published in the series until now, is cast in the frame of reference provided by the concept of enculturation rather than cultural transmission or education. The author is concerned more with how children learn the culture of their social group and with the content of this culture than with how they are taught it. In much of his descriptive analysis, however, the author specifies the ways in which adults, older siblings, and other teachers behave toward children of various age levels. It is largely a matter of emphasis.

The description of Dusun enculturation is as complete as possible within the space limitations of this volume. The author applies in various ways some of the observational categories employed by John and Beatrice Whiting and their associates to extend his basic observations. He is particularly concerned with detailed contextualization and has an interest in cultural patterns and configurations that reflect his own orientation and particularly the influence of Margaret Mead and Douglas Haring, among others.

Notable in this case study is the author's attention to reporting the methods of study used, the provision of a summary of information on the general setting of Dusun enculturation, the analysis of changes occurring in Dusun culture and enculturation, the specification of limitations on the study and its purposes in the context of broader theory and comparative analysis, and the abstraction of ten patterns of enculturation that are offered as a suggestive distillation of the basic processes and as a statement of a configuration of Dusun enculturation. This he provides with the suggestion that the student may find it profitable to utilize these abstracted patterns in comparative studies of the existing literature on enculturation. To this end he supplies a selected bibliography of relevant published studies.

This case study is offered both as a contribution to the growing but underdeveloped scientific literature of enculturation and as a teaching-learning resource for students and instructors in anthropology, psychology, and education.

George and Louise Spindler
General Editors
PORTOLA VALLEY, CALIF., 1969

Acknowledgments

My research on Dusun enculturation was conducted with the assistance of grants from the *National Science Foundation* (grants 5018, 22110) and the *Joint Committee on Asian Studies of the American Council of Learned Societies and the Social Science Research Council* (1959, 1963). Eli Lilly Company and Abbott Laboratories also provided assistance and field supplies. I am solely responsible for the comments and conclusions given here. I was very fortunate to have the friendship and capable assistance of Anthony Gibbon during work in Sensuron. He is Sabah State Senator from Tambunan. Stephen Awong worked with me as an interpreter and field assistant in Baginda and was a friend of worth. I learned much about enculturation from our Dusun friends; O.K.K. G. S. Sundang, formerly Deputy Chief Minister and Minister for Local Government, State of *Sabah*, Malaysia; *O.T.* Dao of Sensuron; *O.T.* Ilos of Baginda; and from *Moshi* of Sensuron and *Kumpiek* and *Dumbor* of Baginda, all skilled ritual specialists. I was given aid and advice by Fathers Putman, Connelly, and Daporz of the Tambunan and Tobo Mill Hill Society Catholic missions. John and Brenda Fryer of the North Borneo Lands and Survey Department were good friends, hosts, and very helpful in our research. My wife Peggy worked and lived under difficult conditions. I owe special thanks to her for her willingness to forego a more comfortable existence. Her courage has been my inspiration. Our sons Rhys and Ian have helped me learn about enculturation. I have benefited in many ways from the works of other scholars on enculturation and socialization, and especially those by Douglas Haring, Margaret Mead, Clyde Kluckhohn, Weston LaBarre, Melford Spiro, John Honigmann, A. I. Hallowell, and Anthony F. C. Wallace. I am, of course, solely responsible for this work. Finally, I know that it was the understanding and patience of our Dusun friends that made it possible for us to learn details of their life.

T.R.W.

Columbus, Ohio
May 1969

Contents

A BORNEO CHILDHOOD
Enculturation in Dusun Society

Introduction

In 1959, accompanied by my wife, I went to North Borneo (now the Malaysian state called *Sabah*) to begin a study of the traditional enculturation process of the Dusun. We resided from August 1959 to August 1960 in Sensuron, a village of 947 persons located in the central mountain jungle highlands. In 1962, with our 13-month-old son, we returned to continue our study in another Dusun community. We resided from September 1962 through August 1963 in Baginda, a village of 751 persons located some 70 road miles south of Sensuron. I have reported on the nature of Dusun culture in a case study (1965), a methods study (1967), and in articles in professional journals (1960, 1961a, 1961b, 1962a, 1962b, 1962c, 1963a, 1963b, 1966, 1968).[1]

It is difficult to compile a bibliographic listing of more than one hundred relatively complete enculturation studies. I would estimate that considerably less than 50 societies have had their enculturation processes adequately described by trained observers.[2]

This fact raises a basic theoretical question. If it is assumed that scientific understanding of the ways humans learn culture is gained best by comparison of data derived from systematic enculturation studies of intact and fully functioning societies, then is not our present ability to make valid statements concerning the socialization process really quite limited?

Much of the available literature of "socialization" confuses, as Mead has noted (1963a), statements about the process of learning culture true of all men (socialization), with statements about the historical particulars true of the ways children learn one culture (enculturation). There is a profound conceptual difference be-

---

[1] Accounts of aspects of Dusun culture by travelers, traders, government officials, and missionaries also are to be found in the works of Antonissen (1958); Evans (1913, 1922, 1923, 1949, 1950, 1951, 1952, 1953, 1954, 1955a,b,c,d,e, 1956); Holley (1955); Luering (1897); Rutter (1922, 1929); Staal (1923–25); White 1955a, 1955b, 1959; Woolley (1932a,b,c, 1936a,b). Glyn-Jones, (1953), Leach (1950), Morris (1966), Wood (1957), and Wood and Moser (1958) have reported on or commented about Dusun society and culture from the bases of their scholarly and anthropological training, field experiences, and concerns. Comparisons of Dusun culture and society with those of other Borneo native groups, such as the Iban and Land Dayak, can be made from the work of Geddes (1954, 1961), Freeman (1955), and Jensen (1965, 1966).

[2] For a bibliography to 1953 of works with partial or complete descriptions of enculturation see Heinicke and B. Whiting (1953). For some references to descriptions of enculturation since 1953 see the bibliography of enculturation studies included in this text and in Haring (1956) and in Honigmann (1967).

tween statements concerning learning human culture and statements about the learning of culture within the context of one society, such as Navaho, Ifugao, Javanese, or Eskimo.

We know a great deal about the ways some American and Western European children learn their local culture. This is very seductive, especially when you consider how little is known concerning the traditional enculturation processes in non-Western, nonliterate, and so-called underdeveloped societies. It is seductive because it may lead us to the logical fallacy of assuming that Western children and Western enculturation processes really represent the prototype of human learning of culture.

In sum, we really know very little that is scientifically meaningful concerning the socialization process because there are so few basic descriptive accounts of enculturation in other, non-Western societies. Many of our "theories" concerning the learning of human culture are no more than speculations, for we have a very inadequate comparative basis to work from in making general statements.

We are fortunate to have had some gifted and articulate individuals concerned with this problem. More than 40 years ago, Ruth Benedict, Margaret Mead, and others perceived the "culture bound," or locally limited, nature of many statements purporting to account for "human" socialization. They pointed out that many such statements really were concerned with man-made patterns of culture historically particular to one society, or a small group of societies in a limited earth region. Later, Ralph Linton, Clyde Kluckhohn, Abram Kardiner, Melville Herskovits, Jules Henry, H. I. Hogbin, A. Irving Hallowell, John W. M. Whiting, John Gillin, Cora DuBois, Weston Labarre, John Honigmann, Laura Thompson, Morris E. Opler, Ernest Beaglehole, Esther Goldfrank, Gregory Bateson, Géza Róheim, George Devereux, and Wayne Dennis, among others, set about trying to illustrate the ways in which data of enculturation illuminate, sharpen and finally validate or make untenable general statements on socialization. Recently Melford Spiro, Anthony F. C. Wallace, Oscar Lewis, Francis L. K. Hsu, Hildred Geertz, Yehudi Cohen, David Landy, William Caudill, Thomas Gladwin, George and Louise Spindler, and the people associated with John and Bernice Whiting in their field studies of enculturation (1963, 1966) have broadened our understanding and appreciation of the ways basic enculturation studies must precede comparative, general studies of socialization.[3]

Despite intensive work by a small number of persons, there still remains an extreme shortage of accurate and reliable descriptions of enculturation. More than 15 years ago John Whiting and I. L. Child (1953:324) made a statement of a similar kind, noting how limited their study of socialization was due to the very few reliable accounts of enculturation available to them at that time. Recently, other persons have made similar statements (see Wallace 1961; Hsu 1961; Kaplan 1961; Cohen 1961, 1964; Kluckhohn, Murray, and Schneider 1953; Barnouw 1963; Honigmann 1967; Goodman 1967; Weinberg 1958; and Mead 1953, 1963a) noting the lack of basic information about enculturation.

The fundamental task of science is the identification and precise description of

---

[3] See the works of Fischer and Fischer (1966), LeVine and LeVine (1966), Maretzki and Maretzki (1966), Minturn and Hitchcock (1966), Nydegger and Nydegger (1966), and Romney and Romney (1966).

the events or objects it seeks to subject to analysis (Haring 1956:107–121). The history of the use of the methods and logic of science in the study of socialization demonstrates that meticulous description and classification of the more gross, directly observable events in the enculturation processes of various local societies has gradually narrowed the limits of the unknown to the point where the intangibles of causal relations and sequences of socialization at least no longer defy tentative formulation and testing on a comparative basis. This has been demonstrated in the works of Whiting and Child (1953) and others.[4] My study of Dusun enculturation is part of the general effort to provide basic data of the kinds that are needed in socialization studies.

I have deliberately tried to refrain from inserting theoretical interpretations of the data. My purpose in this case study is to make clear descriptive statements which summarize and provide a way to understand the configuration of traditional Dusun enculturation.

My wife and I came to know the Dusun as friends. I have tried my best not to allow our subjective biases for things Dusun to enter into this description. However, I must say that we were positively biased toward our subjects. The readers of this text should understand that our culturally structured sympathies for the dependence, openness, trust, and lack of guile of the Dusun children did in some ways structure our descriptive reporting and our observations.

Another source of bias was our own enculturative experience. We learned as we matured within our homes that certain enculturation practices are "right," "natural," "good," and "bad." Thus we were taught that children must be very clean to be in good health, that we were not to respond to hurts and frustrations as a child, but rather as a "big boy" or "big girl," that is, in adult fashion. We learned that physical punishment was "good" for us if we needed it, but bad for our innate dignity and development of our personal character. In short, we acquired hundreds of beliefs, values, conceptions, and judgments about the proper way to raise children as we were being raised. When we were faced daily with Dusun parents raising their children in ways that very often violated the basic beliefs and values by which we were raised, we responded involuntarily to such stimuli in terms of the patterns of our American cultural heritage. We consistently tried to check such responses before they showed through in our facial expressions, posture, a start of motion to help or prevent, or in an exclamation of concern, fear, or disgust. The ability to see oneself behaving in response to novel and strange cultural and social stimuli must be cultivated, worked on, and practiced constantly. It is not an easy skill to master. It is strongly tempting to interfere with a child beating or to take a "dangerous" object, such as a knife, from a toddler. However, then you see yourself behaving as an American adult would, in American terms, and check that response by knowing that in terms of the local culture the "beating" is a principal form of instilling reason and that children are believed to die from accidents whether they play with knives or not; and besides, as one Dusun father put it, "how can you learn to use a knife if you do not use it?"

---

[4] See for instance the discussions of Whiting, Kluckhohn, and Anthony (1958), Whiting and Landauer (1964), Barry (1957), Barry, Bacon, and Child (1957), Barry, Child, and Bacon (1959).

Our primary check upon this bias then was our knowledge that every social form and act is relative to the cultural whole in which it occurs. We reminded ourselves and each other constantly that the things we saw, heard, and talked about with our Dusun neighbors were not "strange" or "unique" to them, were in every instance a part of the whole of Dusun culture, and could not be judged in terms of the meanings of "good" or "bad" in the context of the whole of American culture. This does not mean that we escaped deep involvement entirely as we struggled to force ourselves to look at the events we witnessed in terms of the Dusun culture. The sudden death of a bright, perceptive, and loving three-year-old from disease or accident can cause a heart-wrenching, poignant sense of personal loss.

Finally, I wish to make quite explicit the fact that I have chosen here to stress the traditional patterns of Dusun enculturation. I did not choose to present a discussion essentially concerned with the changes which are occurring in Dusun enculturation because of contacts between Dusun and members of Malay, Chinese, Indian, European, and other societies, or because of the impact of the new political organization of the area under Malaysia. In several sections of this text (see Chapters 1, 2, and 7) I have acknowledged and documented many of the changes that have been occurring in traditional Dusun enculturation. I have chosen to stress the traditional patterns of Dusun enculturation in this case study in order to contribute to the fund of comparative materials showing the great diversity of human child raising and education.

The text which follows begins with a chapter describing the general setting of Dusun enculturation. The second chapter briefly discusses the specific methods used in this study. The next three chapters recount the events of a Dusun child's enculturation. Chapter 6 summarizes and briefly discusses the patterns comprising the configuration of traditional Dusun enculturation. The last chapter of the text describes some of the changes which are taking place in patterns of Dusun enculturation. Suggested readings about enculturation processes in other societies follow the last chapter.

1 / The setting of enculturation

A NUMBER OF FEATURES which are a vital part of the setting of traditional Dusun enculturation are described in this chapter. A brief summary account is given of the Dusun people, their natural environment, and the traditional system of Dusun culture. The chapter also contains a description of the events which occurred in the period between 1881 and 1963 as a formal educational system developed in the country of North Borneo. The chapter concludes with comments intended to demonstrate the outlines of the changes which are taking place in the Dusun world. This discussion is intended to serve as an introduction to the description of traditional Dusun enculturation in the following chapters.

THE PEOPLE

The Dusun are predominantly *Indo-Malayan* in appearance.[1] Individual Dusun often have wavy or straight dark hair, with deep nose roots and broad nose tips. Men often have slight brow ridges and women usually have well-developed breasts. Their skin color varies from yellow to dark brown, depending on exposure to the sun. Their eyes are dark brown with a slight inner eyefold. They have little face or body hair. *Indo-Malayans* are short in stature, with men usually under 5 feet, 6 inches and women often under 5 feet, 3 inches in height. Both Dusun males and females tend to have thick-chested, lean, and well-muscled bodies.

Dusun speak a language, divided into over half-dozen local dialects, of the Austronesian (Malayo-Polynesian) language stock.[2] Today Dusun use a variety of loan words which have been borrowed from long-term contacts with Indians, Chinese, Arabs, Malays, and Europeans. Some Malay is spoken by many Dusun since it has been a "trade" and "school" language. Many Dusun living in isolated areas do not speak Malay regularly or well.

---

[1] See Coon (1965:177–185) for one phenotypic description of Indo-Malayan peoples. Studies of blood-group frequencies indicate that Borneo Indo-Malayan peoples are typified by a higher frequency of gene I^B at the ABO locus, a higher frequency of gene L^M than L^N, and a total lack of the Kell positive factor and the I^{A2} allele. At the Rh gene locus there is a high frequency of R^I and a reported absence of the r gene (Hulse 1963:266–421; Livingstone 1967:183–184; Lie-Injo Luan Eng, J. Chin and T. S. Ti 1964; F. Vella and D. Tavaria 1961).

[2] The languages of the Austronesian phylum conventionally are divided into (1) Indonesian, (2) Polynesian, (3) Melanesian, and (4) Micronesian. Dusun belongs to the North Indonesian subgroup of Philippine languages (Cense and Unlenbeck 1958:25; Dyen 1965:31).

THE LAND

Dusun live in a natural world of great beauty. It is a world quite unlike the one known to most Americans or Europeans. Much of the land has been created as it was sharply thrust up out of warm Eocene, Oligocene, and Miocene seas. About two million years before the present, more land was formed as the glaciers of the northern hemisphere locked up great amounts of sea water into ice formations. This process led to the lowering of the seas about Borneo by an estimated average of 240 feet. For part of the very long period of the Pleistocene (about two million years) Borneo was joined to the mainland of Asia and a land bridge probably existed between Borneo and the present island of Palawan. Then, great flooding rivers draining the heart of Southeast Asia cut through the massive blocks of Borneo's sharply folded rocks. In the time of the Pleistocene there were many thousands of years when intense rains wore heavily at much of the exposed rock. The rains and flooding rivers broke down rock to create a thick layer of heavy soil over much of the lowest land in Borneo.

By the time the ancestors of the modern Dusun arrived in northern Borneo (perhaps sometime between 1500 and 1000 B.C.) the land of the central and western area was composed of many small steep-sided valleys surrounded by jagged peaks of mountains rising 5000 to 8000 feet and dominated by the towering heights of *Mount Kinabalu*. This great hulking monolith of igneous rock rises approximately 13,455 feet over the land.

Today much of northern Borneo is covered by highly varied soils which change in thickness and type in the short distances from a valley floor to nearby hillsides and mountainsides. Much of this soil is of a deep, reddish type called *lateritic*.

This tortuously formed land, with its complex undulations, is generally covered below 2000 feet by a lush tropical rain forest of thickly growing, broad-leaved, high evergreen trees. Many woody creepers and other climbing plants cling to and festoon the great trunks of the rain forest trees. These trees rise from massive flaring bases to thick trunks ending in a canopy of leaves at 100 to 120 feet above the ground. At the foot of these forest giants are ferns rising among a profusion of smaller plants whose numbers and density in some places comprise a thousand different kinds in an area of a few square miles. The floor of the rain forest is covered by a thick, soft, springy, wet layer of litter which is made up of decaying plant material. Where the primary forest has been cut down by Dusun, low, small trees and heavy vines soon grow up into nearly impassable thickets. In some areas of heavy cultivation of the forest, heavy rain falling on the lateritic soils has produced, by leaching, small areas of open grasslands covered with high, sharp-edged grasses. In the elevations from 2000 to 4000 feet the rain forest gives way to trees of the oak and chestnut type. Above 4000 feet there are low gnarled trees, mosses, grasses, and varieties of shrubs.

This land is subjected to an annual climate of high temperature and humidity, heavy and violent rains and turbulent winds. These factors of climate are tempered by the different altitudes of the land causing relief contrasts in intensity of amounts of heat, rain, winds, and sunlight. Depending on the cloud cover, temperatures may range in the extremes in the lowland forests from 68 to 95°F and from 55 to 92°F in mountain areas above 2000 feet. Local annual rainfall in the two monsoon seasons (November–March; April–October) may be between 60 and 160 inches, depending on the land forms. Heavy rains often are limited to a local area because of mountain barriers to movement of wet, low clouds. On occasion, 5 to 10 inches of rain fall in a few hours at one point, while very little rain falls 10 miles away. This leads to abrupt changes in local stream levels. Some large rivers rise in a few hours to 30 feet above their normal levels. Such flooding causes steep-sided high stream and river banks. Borneo highland streams are placid, clear, ankle-deep waterways one hour, then change in the next to roaring torrents of muddy water, tumbling great uprooted trees over and over into large boulders with gushes of spray and shellfire-like noises. In the higher elevations, the streams usually are cool, often dropping to 65°F in the early mornings. At the two times a year (March, October) when the monsoon winds change direction, there may be localized dry spells of two weeks to a month. Then there are very high temperatures. The grasslands dry, stream levels fall sharply, and the rain forest begins to wither and dry when the intense sunlight in a cloudless sky penetrates the leafy canopy.

Then in an abrupt change the first rains of the monsoon come on violent winds whose gusts sometimes reach short bursts of hurricane force, carrying stinging sheets of blinding rain across the land in deafening roars. The jungle turns into a slippery morass of mud, constantly dripping vegetation, and a misted world of such high humidity that mold, decay, and mildew are everywhere.

As the cycle of weather progresses to the next dry spell, the violent rainstorms become days and sometimes a week of rains causing streams to flood and the land to become saturated. Then there is a period of several months with hot, damp mornings and afternoon thundershowers. In the months of afternoon thunderstorms, great rolling crescendos of noise echo across the sodden, dark skies, which are laced with sudden lightning flashes. Brilliant and intensely hued rainbows may arch out from mountain peaks to valley floors in these days and sometimes compete with sunsets of breathtaking clarity of golds, reds, and purples spreading across the jagged horizon.

In the higher elevations, heavy early morning mist and ground fog is common. Here, the air temperature drops rapidly in the night hours, while humidity remains nearly constant. This results in chilly nights and mornings. When the winds blow in the early days of the monsoons the higher elevations of northern Borneo are extremely uncomfortable from the constant damp cold that lasts nearly the entire day.

The wet jungle forests covering this mountain land are the home of a great variety of animals. There are more than 79 species of freshwater fishes and 200 species of reptiles and amphibians, including large lizards, cobras, pythons, frogs, and turtles. Gliding and flying animals are common, with some 500 species of birds and a variety of squirrel that glides in leaps from tree to tree in the forest canopy. There are numerous kinds of bats, including those that live by eating fruit and some with "wing" spans of up to 2 feet across. There is a profusion of kinds and sizes of butterflies of bright hues. Monkeys and gibbons are found in the rain-forest canopy. The orangutan is found in the northern Borneo lowland jungles. The forest floor contains uncounted types of ants, insects, and leeches.

Mosquito, fly, flea, and tick populations are numerous and widespread. Larger animals of the forest include deer, bear, pig, wild oxen, wildcats, and pangolin. Large saltwater crocodiles are found in the rivers near the sea. These waters also contain poisonous snakes.

The mosquito, fly, flea, and tick populations are carriers of the diseases of malaria, cholera, plague, and typhus. Human life is also endangered by the presence of more than 25 types of poisonous snakes, the prevalence of harmful stinging and biting insects, by the crocodile and the python, the world's largest land snake.

When a Dusun moves about in this world he travels across a landscape that demands his full exertion and attention. Movement through the primary forest is slow because of the steep slopes and due to the difficulty of walking on slippery paths. On such paths a fall can lead to death from a drop down a slope to the rocks of a stream far below. A Dusun just emerging from the forest can be identified easily: his legs and feet are often spotted with many small bleeding wounds from leech bites, while his arms and legs may be crisscrossed with long bloody scratches torn by sharp, thorny trailing vines, and his clothes will be wet and muddy from falls and fording streams. He may carry a 4- to 5-foot length of rattan vine, fashioned into a cane to aid in descending steep slopes and crossing flooded streams. Often, he will have red blotches on his body from an intensely burning rash caused by contact with small jungle plants.

THE TRADITIONAL CULTURE

Dusun share a system of learned and patterned conventional understandings, manifest in act and artifact, which have been transmitted to them from the preceding generations. These are summarized below as a general background to the discussion of traditional Dusun enculturation.

Most Dusun now live in small, separate family dwellings. Houses usually are made of split bamboo walls, floors, with bamboo or palm thatch roofs and are set up 3 to 4 feet from the ground on hardwood posts. A contemporary Dusun community contains from 10 to 200 such separate houses, often closely packed into a small space at the edge of rice fields. In the recent past, Dusun often lived in structures which have been called "longhouses." A Dusun longhouse was marked by its length, a common roof covering all the nuclear-family household apartments within it and a public veranda along the front of individual households. It was constructed of the same materials used in today's Dusun houses and was also set upon hardwood posts. Each compartment of a longhouse was occupied by a nuclear family, that is, a father and a mother and their dependent children. Sometimes a newly married son and his bride, an aged grandparent, or other relative also lived with the nuclear family. A typical longhouse consisted of from 10 to 30 nuclear families. Contemporary Dusun houses usually are occupied by nuclear families and sometimes include an aged or dependent relative.

Dusun traditionally made their tools from bamboo, selected jungle hardwoods, rattan vines, and from stone, bone, and fired clay. They have long used some tools with parts of metal such as knives, spears, hoes, and the like. The Dusun use the

Women drying rice after harvest; woman in the right background is cutting fire-wood. Bamboo poles are sweeps to fend off domestic animals from the grain.

natural world in three ways to gain their living: (1) agriculture, (2) hunting and gathering of foods, and (3) gathering of raw materials for manufacture of clothing, shelter, and tools.

The primary crop grown by Dusun is rice, cultivated in one of two forms: (1) *swidden rice* ("dry" or "hill" rice) and (2) wet rice ("irrigated" rice). Rice agriculture traditionally has been a shifting swidden cultivation on mountainsides cleared by cutting and burning jungle vegetation. Most Dusun rice agriculture today is wet-rice cultivation of flat areas along streams and on plains between mountains and along seacoasts, where the abundant fresh water can be used to irrigate the rice crop. Some *swidden rice* is also grown by villagers subsisting primarily on wet-rice cultivation. Dusun consider rice as "the one good food," "the best food," and "the proper ceremonial food." Daily life in a Dusun village is organized about an annual agriculture calendar for preparing fields, planting, weeding, making agricultural tools, and harvesting of rice. Hunting and major manufacturing activities usually occur when time is available in the round of agricultural work, especially in the weeks after harvest and before the time of planting a new crop of rice. Depending on the soil and location of the field, nuclear families may spend about 57 days per year per adult member in preparing and planting 2 to 5 acres of wet rice to try to secure the 300 gallons (dry measure) of rice for food and the 195 gallons of rice for feeding animals said to be necessary to sustain a family of two adults and three children. Approximately one-quarter of the nuclear families in the two villages of Sensuron and Baginda in 1959–1960 and 1962–1963 did not secure enough wet

9

rice to meet the requirements Dusun feel necessary to maintain life at an adequate physical and social level. To try to secure more rice, most of these families cleared and planted small swidden rice fields. Most households prepare and plant gardens for raising more than 25 other types of foodstuffs. Among these foods are the sweet potato, greater yam, and manioc, which often are planted in quantity as major supplements to rice in daily eating. Dusun also cultivate trees and shrubs bearing edible fruits, including, among many others, coconut, banana, breadfruit, mango, papaya, and citrus fruits. Many other plants are cultivated in gardens or in areas near the house for use as material for manufacturing and for cash sale. These include bamboo, cotton, gourds, indigo, derris, rubber, coffee, and pepper.

The diet gained by agricultural activities is extended by hunting in the jungle. Most animals of the jungle are hunted for food. These include the pig, deer, bear, gibbon, orangutan, and monkey. Traps of bamboo and rattan, the spear, poison dart and blowpipe, packs of specially trained dogs and recently shotguns are used as hunting tools. Fishing and gathering of marine animals are conducted by use of tools of bamboo, fiber, and poisons. A wide variety of natural materials also are regularly collected by Dusun from the jungle for use as food and in the making of tools, clothing, and shelter. These items include rattan, bamboo, hardwoods, tree barks, fruits, vegetables, insects, worms, and many small animals.

A number of types of domestic animals are used by Dusun as sources of food, power, and raw materials. Chickens, pigs, ducks, geese, water buffalo, dogs, and cats now are common in a Dusun village. Several of these animals, including the pig, chicken, and water buffalo, have important uses in ritual activities. The water buffalo is a key source of labor power in preparing wet-rice fields.

The Dusun live in a natural world which they define as having distinct aspects. They believe these aspects are controlled by helpful and harmful forces and beings. A complex story of the creation of the universe, man, and all living things provides a setting for many Dusun beliefs and actions. Dusun are anxious about certain events which they define as crises. Birth, sickness, death, individual fortune, success in hunting, yield of crops, outcomes of personal arguments, flood, drought, epidemic disease, and war are all conceived as crises happenings. Dusun often seek to deal with such crises through the activities of specialists in ritual behavior. Both male and female specialists attempt to divine the nature of a specific crisis, undo unfortunate events, restore events to their original conditions, prevent sickness, and provide protection against impending harm. Ritual specialists are important people in a Dusun community since they know the many complex details of proper ways to deal with the many different spirit beings, forces, and supernatural agencies which can cause or help prevent life crises. Much of Dusun life is involved with ritual activities conducted by specialists for afflicted persons. Individuals also use rituals on their own behalf. Dusun pay particular attention to omens as indicators of impending change in personal and community fortune which foreshadows crises. Omens are taken from the sights and sounds of particular jungle animals, occurrence of unusual events (such as a green tree branch falling), the contents of dreams, and the accidental finding of special objects. Certain numbers and words are taken to have omen content in particular situations. A great amount of attention is given by Dusun to conserving and extending their personal fortune. Many magical acts and social practices are used to insure that a personal store of luck, which is acquired at birth, is not diminished. Dusun feel they can extend their luck through successful farming, hunting, trading, and the winning of personal disputes.

Dusun arrange social relationships with one another in a series of groupings that encompass most daily events. The basic social unit is the nuclear-family household. In Sensuron, households are grouped into several divisions on a territorial basis. These groupings have mutual aid, ceremonial, and, formerly, military functions. The most functional social group having a specific territorial dimension is an association of particular nuclear-family households within a neighborhood. This group (*timbaŋ*) functions also as a mutual aid, ceremonial, and political unit.[3] In times of crises arising from accident, disease, death, natural disaster, and warfare members of a *timbaŋ* work together to deal with the problem. Older men of a *timbaŋ* may comprise an informal council to hear disputes. The fighting unit in war was often composed of *timbaŋ* men.

In addition to social groups based on territorial associations there is a specific social group (*senåkågun*) which is derived from recognition by its members that each is a descendant of a particular ancestor whose activities are told in legend and folktale on special occasions of feasting, and in whose name some land is owned and special rituals are conducted. This group is an ancestor-oriented social entity that depends on links of relationship to the common ancestor in each generation, acquired through either parent and not through relationships to one particular person. In Sensuron all members of the community belonged to one *senåkågun*. Members of other villages may belong to this same *senåkågun*. There probably are five to seven *senåkågun* in Dusun society. These groups regulate marriage to the extent that members usually have married within the *senåkågun*. They also have practiced ownership (*sågeån*) of some land, fruit trees, jars, gongs, weapons, and ritual paraphernalia. A leader of a *senåkågun* has been selected in each generation by public discussion and general consent of group members. This leader has settled disputes, arranged ritual for the group, and taken an active part in discussing and directing economic, political, and social matters of the group. Differences between these groups have been marked by dialect, food habits, particular behavior forms, and styles of music, dance, and decorative arts.

A second social group without a territorial base is composed of persons acknowledging their relationship to a particular individual without regard to whether the relationship is through a male or female relative. From the point of view of a Dusun individual membership in this group (*teŋran*) is comprised ideally of that group of living relatives from great-grandparents through seventh cousins in the father's line of descent and from great-grandparents to third cousins in the mother's line of descent, with inclusion of all persons married to relatives in these classes. Actually, membership in the *teŋran* today is counted only within the range of third cousins in both lines of descent. This group defines the social range beyond which a marriage partner must be selected, and is the social unit of most importance beyond the nuclear family. The link between *teŋran* which occurs at marriage is considered

---

[3] The orthographic style used here is described in detail in the Linguistic Chart, and in Williams (1963a:181). This style is commensurate with the International Phonetic Alphabet symbols rendered in an orthographic chart of Dusun voccoids and nonvoccoids in Williams (1962b:156).

by Dusun a vital social fact, for it is the two *teŋran* groups of his parents which include a child's circle of closest relatives beyond his nuclear family; these are the relatives a child must depend on in times of a crisis if his parents cannot effectively cope with the situation.

Social relations within territorially and kinship-based groups are established and maintained generally through use of special terms which carry emotional meanings for their users. These terms are basic to a system of meanings and associated patterns of behavior that define rights, duties, and concerns of the individual in day-to-day and special social situations. Those used for talking with and about relatives have special forms and are of particular types.

Material possessions in Dusun life are associated with the social system through a set of beliefs that link things to people. These beliefs comprise a large number of patterns concerning types of ownership of property and means of acquisition, exchange, or disposal of property. Things are treated by Dusun as either movable or immovable in nature. Dusun say there are ten classes of movable property and two classes of immovable property. All property is said by Dusun to have a personal history composed of "life experiences" of "birth" by manufacture or in natural events, a "life" of unique experiences and a "death" in sale, consumption, or destruction. There are complex social rules for borrowing, exchange, and inheritance of property. Marriage involves a substantial exchange of property. Dusun give much attention to property and its meanings, and define the prestige of persons and some social events according to the types of property owned, used, destroyed, or consumed. Dusun beliefs concerning acquisition, keeping, and loss of property are linked directly to conceptions of life crises and good and bad fortune.

There have been two means of controlling and using power and authority in traditional Dusun society: (1) customary law and (2) war. Customary law consists of a series of ideas concerning peaceful settlement of disputes arising over property, claims of alteration of fortune, and disagreements concerning acts such as adultery and incest. Social power in Dusun society has rested upon the factors of sex, age, property, personal knowledge, and reputation for adherence to customary law. A wise and wealthy older man who is respected by his neighbors is often a powerful person. Customary law operates with reference to detailed tests of truth, public hearings, and conceptions of some 58 offenses grouped by Dusun into the classes of: (1) offenses against the person, (2) sex and marriage offenses, (3) property offenses, (4) fraud, (5) social offenses, and (6) religious offenses. Hearings concerning violations of customary law usually have been concerned with secular rather than religious offenses. Property, sex, and social offense hearings were most common in the villages of Sensuron and Baginda during the time of our residence. Customary law hearings have been conducted by the neighborhood *timbaŋ* council on minor offenses; major offenses have been heard by a village council of the community leader and the senior members of the several neighborhood councils. In the past, punishments have ranged from small fines to death or banishment from the community. Now, "serious" problems are turned over to the district officer and local police.

Political activity in Dusun life has centered upon the persons possessed of the most power to insure compliance with their wishes. Older men in control of great amounts of property and skilled as hunters, warriors, or ritual specialists and with a reputation of knowing details of traditional law have been the most politically powerful persons in a community. When customary law did not apply to a situation, force in the form of warfare was applied to correct a situation viewed as harmful. In the past, if a stranger had acted in a manner harmful to the good fortune of the village, usually it would not have been possible under customary law to punish him. A war party of young men would set out to deal with the offender through killing him in a quick raid on the other village. Often many other persons were killed in these raids. The community which had been raided frequently would send a war party to right the damage to their good fortune which was caused by the raid on their community. This counterraid often led to another raid and counterraid and to a long-term state of chronic warfare in which persons were ambushed by a war party to balance the last offense against the fortune of a community. Such raids no longer take place. War parties usually took head and hand trophies from victims as symbols of restoring fortune to their lives. Trophies were kept and displayed in rituals which are believed to help keep community and personal fortune in balance.

There were decorative and representational art forms in use in Dusun life, made in naturalistic carvings of wood utensils and house doors and in symbolic designs woven into cloth, hats, and baskets. Vocal and instrumental music, dancing, and verse recitations also were vital parts of Dusun life.

Dusun values concerning relations between man and nature appear dominated by a belief that men must submit to or try to balance most natural events, such as floods, rains, drought, rather than to seek to prevent them. Dusun generally are oriented to the past as a guide for judgments regarding present or future behavior, and Dusun usually believe that the ties which unite persons in a nuclear-family household are primary in all situations involving inheritance of land, personal property, and authority. Behavior in the nuclear-family unit is believed properly individualistic with each adult responsible to himself in matters involving other nuclear-family members. Behavior outside the nuclear family is judged to be governed best by social arrangements which make individuals kin. If no arrangements of this nature can be established, the relations between persons are believed best based on customary law. If relations between persons cannot be established through kinship or customary law, there has been little chance of common social action.

ASPECTS OF VILLAGE LIFE[4]

Daily life in a Dusun community includes a variety of events which are vital aspects of the world most Dusun children learn to know and deal with effectively.

---

[4] It is important to note that most likely a Dusun would not select the aspects of village life reported here as "meaningful" or even worth comment, since they form a basic part of his "natural world," which he senses through culturally structured perceptions shaped and directed by his experiences in the Dusun enculturation process.

First, there are the physical stimuli of the jungle smells of mold, mildew, and decay intermingling with the odors of decaying animal and human wastes and the pungent aromas of curing and pickled meats. And there also are the natural stimuli that come from the thickly misted mornings, the damp and chilly mountain breezes, the turgid and dark rain clouds of afternoons and the opaque dimness of humid and hot middays. The hues of green vegetation, unrelieved except for an occasional splash of color of flowers near a house, or by the transient golds of rice near harvest, provide a pervading sense of color best described as murky, obscure, and faint.

Paths and walkways between houses usually are ankle deep in mud and water. The mud often is warm from the sun and fetid in smell from wastes thrown from the houses. For much of the year movement in a Dusun village involves walking in an ankle-deep mixture of wet mud and waste.

A general pandemonium from noise of work activities, people talking, shouting, and singing, and from the calls of domestic animals comprises another aspect of village life for the maturing Dusun child. Most of the day a community resounds with an uproar of calls of chickens, ducks, pigs, dogs, water buffalo, and geese, mixed with noises of an incessant chopping, pounding, and grinding from work tasks, and the overriding chorus of the songs, shouts, and calls of children at play. Adults add to this background of village noises in giving long, piercing yells to summon family members from work in the field or forests. At night a Dusun village pulsates with sounds of life as people snore, cough, and spit, or sit talking before the house fire pit.

During harvest and periods of major rituals nights throb with the deep resounding echoes of gongs and the clatter of the rhythmic thumping of small wood and deerhide drums played in a dozen houses to a half-dozen tunes. Sounds of gongs from distant villages often blend into local gong tunes and are a background for the wail of a solitary bamboo flute. These patterns of sound blend into distinct modes, so that many Dusun come to be able to sense a shift of events in daily life by major changes in levels, intensity, and types of sounds in the community.

Another aspect of Dusun village life is the way village space is used and the ways Dusun regulate personal and social distance. The jungle-clad mountains about villages rise sharply against the sky. The community often is crowded in its physical setting among the mountains. Houses and rice-storage structures run down a slope with little space to walk between them. The people of the village are in constant physical contact with each other. Dusun touch each other in crowds with arms, knees, elbows, or in some manner to give body contact.

And Dusun life has an active tempo. This comes from a heightened attention to movement and a precision of motion in work and leisure. People are busy at their work tasks. They move with briskness and give an impression of being thoroughly occupied, reacting quickly in work acts; a knife is not allowed just to bounce back when a man chops at a tree. It is pulled back from the cutting stroke with force and dispatch. Dusun stride briskly in a short, choppy walk. They are very attentive to the world about them. There is an acute awareness of motion and sound. This leads to a tempo of daily life that best is characterized in European and American terms as "restless," "powerful," "intense," and "vigorous."

CHANGES IN EDUCATION, 1881–1963

The Dusun have been in contact with other cultural traditions for a very long period of time. Scattered archaeological data and historical documents tend to show that from about the fifth or sixth century B.C. through the fifteenth century A.D. there were contacts between the native peoples of Borneo and representatives of other cultural traditions, including Indians, Chinese, and Arabs. There is no certain way of knowing whether the Dusun were in regular, first-hand contact with members of these other cultures. It is likely that changes in Dusun culture took place because of new ways brought to Borneo by members of these other cultural traditions. However by the time the first Europeans came to Borneo in the early sixteenth century, most Dusun culture configurations probably were as they had been for hundreds of years previously. It may be that the enculturation process in Dusun society was little affected by contacts with Indian, Chinese, and Arabic cultures or initial contacts with European cultures.

After the British government granted a royal charter to the North Borneo Company in 1881, changes began which would eventually affect the configuration of Dusun enculturation.[5] In the 64-year period between 1881 and the end of World War II there were efforts by the government of North Borneo to provide education for people native to the country. However, in the time between 1881 and 1921 education for the natives of North Borneo generally was left by the government to Catholic and Protestant missionary groups. A government school for the sons of "native chiefs" was established in 1881 by the first governor. The school closed in 1887. That same year small Catholic mission schools were operating on both the west and east coasts of the country. In 1888 the first Protestant mission school was opened. About 1900 the government began to pay a small subsidy to mission schools for support of formal education. In 1909 the government created a "department of education" to dispense and supervise the subsidies. In 1913 the mission schools had a reported total of 753 pupils with government grants totaling $2672 Straits dollars (about $890 U.S. dollars).

At this time the majority of students in mission schools were Chinese. Between 1890 and 1915 great numbers of Chinese laborers were brought from China to North Borneo to work timber and rubber estates. By 1913 some Dusun children were attending Catholic mission schools located near their home villages on the western coastal plain of the country. There were probably no more than 100 Dusun students in school at this date.

In 1915 the government established another school for sons of native chiefs. This school was founded on the belief that it would be easier to administer the country if the government trained the sons who were to inherit their father's political powers. By 1918 there were 12 students in this school, with ages ranging from 9 to 25 years. The training was conducted in Malay, termed the "vernacular language" by the

---

[5] For a history of North Borneo see K. G. Tregonning, 1958, *Under Chartered Company Rule,* Singapore, University of Malaya Press (revised in 1965 under the title *A History of Sabah*).

government. The course of studies consisted of teaching the students to read and write Malay at a primary-grade level. This school was closed in 1930 when it finally became apparent to the government that the reasoning on which the school effort was based was in error; leadership has not been a hereditary right among native groups in North Borneo.

In 1921, under pressures exerted by some native leaders, the North Borneo government started three Malay language "vernacular schools" which were supposed to be open to all local children. The vernacular schools grew by 1930 to ten primary schools with about 391 students. The pupils were mostly boys between the ages of 6 and 15 years. Some girls were enrolled in these schools after 1930, but were formally banned in 1936 by the governor, who found himself uncertain of the values of coeducation for natives and unwilling to spend money to build separate schools for girls. There were probably about one-hundred Dusun students in vernacular schools in 1930.

By 1940 there were 28 primary vernacular schools with 1663 students. Perhaps 40 percent of these pupils were Dusun. The course of studies at this time consisted of classes in reading and writing Malay, extensive physical training, and gardening, with a little time devoted to local geography, simple arithmetic, and personal hygiene. In 1940 there were also 52 primary-grade mission schools with 3992 students. The course of studies in the mission schools was conducted generally in English and consisted of subjects to be found in a traditional European and English primary education system: reading, writing, spelling, arithmetic, geography, world history, literature, simple physical science, and the arts, including some music, drawing, and painting. In 1940 somewhat less than 30 percent of mission-school students were Dusun.

In 1940 there were also 59 Chinese-language primary schools with some 4779 students. These schools were organized by local Chinese communities. The course of studies in the Chinese schools was designed to produce scholars, teachers, and government officials and included extensive training in the reading and writing of classic logograms and in traditional Chinese literature and philosophy.

In 1940 there were three separate primary school systems in operation in North Borneo. These comprised some 139 schools with about 10,434 students, which were supported by grants of government funds amounting to $40,279 Straits dollars (about $13,426 U.S. dollars). The total number of Dusun children in these schools was very small compared to the numbers of children from other ethnic groups in the country and in proportion to the number of school-aged (5 to 18 years) Dusun children. By estimate, in 1940 considerably less than 15 percent of all Dusun children were being educated in primary schools. This figure, as an estimate for the entire Dusun school-age population, must be qualified by the fact that most Dusun pupils were boys and were in mission schools and vernacular schools on the west coastal plain. There were very few Dusun children in school in the interior areas of the country. Since the Dusun population was concentrated in the mountain interior of North Borneo, this meant that in 1940 most Dusun children were still being enculturated in traditional ways. However the bases for later change in Dusun culture and enculturation were being set in even these very limited numbers of children attending schools. Some Dusun children were being trained in ways which had little to do with everyday life in a Dusun village. The education in a mission or vernacular school broke the continuity between Dusun culture and the educational experiences of Dusun children. The educators were male and female foreigners, often German, Dutch, Irish, Scots, or English, and sometimes Malays and Chinese. Dusun children became passive subjects listening to the proper ways to deal with a world and a technology they had never seen. Many school hours were spent by Dusun children learning to write and spell "apple" and "sheep" when the children had no conception of such entities, and the European school system, particularly as it was used in mission schools, was based on a view of man which centered on the individual and strongly emphasized self-reliance. This view of man is one which increasingly divides individuals in their social relations by stressing their personal ambitions to achieve statuses of power and wealth. This European world view also stressed belief in a rapidly changing culture and society as a normal and desirable condition. These attitudes about man, culture, and society are very different from those learned by Dusun children in the traditional process of enculturation. Dusun view man as dependent upon persons related by ties of kinship or friendship. This view of man holds that individuals should be drawn into ever closer social and personal relations. This world view also stresses long-term stability in culture and society as a normal and desirable condition. In addition to being presented with very divergent views of man in their homes and in the schools, the children were often subjected to attitudes of their teachers, which held that the Dusun culture and social life were "inferior," "primitive," and "uncivilized" and of little worth when compared to Western European ways and culture.

The Japanese invasion and the Allied reoccupation of North Borneo in World War II caused the physical destruction of most school buildings, the death of many teachers, and an almost total breakdown of the formal educational system. The quick replacement of European administrators by the Japanese invaders also called into open question the natural superiority of European culture and set the stage for new political activities that would later accelerate the changes in Dusun life.

In 1946 the 65-year rule of the royally chartered North Borneo Company ended and the country became a British colony. In the years from 1946 until 1963, when North Borneo became a state in the new nation of Malaysia, the system and style of formal education was changed little from the time prior to World War II. In this 17 years there was an extensive rebuilding of schools and sporadic government attempts to bring more of the country's children into schools. And there was a continuation of the three-part (mission, vernacular, Chinese) school system, supported by government grants. By 1960, under Colonial administration, there were 45,777 students in 319 primary schools, 15 secondary schools, and 1 teacher-training school. These schools were supported in 1960 by government grants of $4,245,793 Straits dollars (about $1,415,264 U.S. dollars). Even with this rate of growth between 1940 and 1960 in the number of schools, pupils, and amount of funds spent, however, still more than 70 percent of the total school-age population of North Borneo was not attending any type of school in 1960. The reporting tables for the 1960 North Borneo census show that there was a total of 6465 Dusun children in schools of all types on the day of the census.[6] This total, which includes 4459 boys and 2006 girls, is approximately 14 percent of the total 45,777 students of all ethnic groups enrolled in North Borneo schools on census day, 1960. And this number of Dusun children is approximately 13 percent of the 47,753 school-aged (5 to 19 years) Dusun children on the day of the 1960 census. This sharply contrasts with the total enrollment of Chinese students on the 1960 census day; then, Chinese students comprised approximately 66 percent or 30,270 students of the total 45,777 North Borneo students of all ethnic groups in school on census day. And this number of Chinese students is 74 percent of the approximately 40,878 Chinese children of school age on census day, 1960.

The figures of the 1960 census also show that of the 6465 Dusun children in schools, 6162 were enrolled in primary schools, 250 were enrolled in secondary schools, and 53 were enrolled in the teacher-training institution. These data become more meaningful when put in terms of the percentage of total school enrollment; 14 percent of all North Borneo primary students were Dusun, 6 percent of secondary students were Dusun, and 21 percent of the teacher-training students were Dusun. On the census day in 1960, 65 percent of all primary students were Chinese, 83 percent of all secondary students were Chinese, and 52 percent of all teacher-training students were Chinese.

In 1960 the impact of formal education on traditional patterns of enculturation was greater than it had been prior to World War II. Yet even in 1960 the total numbers of Dusun children being affected by these changes were still a small proportion of all children in Dusun culture.[7] It is accurate to say that considerably more than half of all Dusun children in school in 1960 were in schools on the North Borneo coastal plains. As an example, in 1959–1960 in the village of Sensuron in the interior of North Borneo there were 230 school-aged boys and girls in the total village population of 947 persons. There was a vernacular primary school at Kinaban (founded in 1951), 2 miles from the village, and a mission primary school at Toboh (founded in 1934), 4 miles from the community. The vernacular school was run as a "day school," that is, all children returned to their homes after each day of school. The mission primary school was operated as a boarding school by two European Catholic priests and three European nuns. There were two Dusun teachers at the vernacular school.

The number of village children attending the vernacular school in 1959–1960 varied between 18 and 30; of these children, 20 were boys and 10 were girls. A small group of 11 children went to the vernacular school nearly every day. Another

---

[6] See, *North Borneo, Report on the Census of Population taken on 10th August, 1960*, L. W. Jones, ed., Kuching, Sarawak, Government Printing Office, March 1962, p. 302. Hereafter cited as *North Borneo, Report on the Census.*

[7] Census reporting (Table 12-b, p. 220, *North Borneo, Report on the Census*) gives figures for "Dusun Aged 10 and over by Sex, Age and Level of Education Completed." These data show that if persons over ten years of age are considered in the total Dusun population of 145,229 in 1960, which is a total of 96,216 individuals, only 9818 have had education of any type. This is approximately 10 percent of the population over ten years of age. This contrasts with the Chinese (see Table 12-f, p. 224, *North Borneo, Report on the Census*), where 43,377 persons, or approximately 63 percent of the 68,849 Chinese individuals aged ten and over had schooling of some type.

group of 6 children went to the vernacular school infrequently, on the order of one or two days in a five-day school week. There were 13 children who were absent from classes between one and three days in any particular week. Among the remainder of the 230 school-aged village children, one girl boarded at the nearby mission school and attended class there regularly. Two boys were in a Catholic mission school on the east coastal plain. However, the remainder of the village children received no regular schooling.[8]

A CHANGING DUSUN WORLD

The Dusun are the largest native society in Sabah, numbering 145,229 persons among a total native population of 306,448, in a total population of 454,421 individuals (Jones 1962). Until World War II the majority of Dusun were isolated from the many changes taking place in the rest of the world and in the few coastal towns of North Borneo. The Japanese invasion of North Borneo in 1942, a harsh occupation, and bitter fighting to free the country resulted in most Dusun being thrust into regular contact with individuals behaving in very different ways. The re-establishment of civil government under the direct supervision of the British Colonial office brought the Dusun further into the mainstream of change in the country. New roads, air services, and communication networks by radio, telephone, and mail contributed to a rapid postwar growth of trade into and within the country.

In the summer of 1959, when we arrived in Jesselton, now Kota Kinabalu, the capital of the colony of North Borneo, we flew from Singapore as two of the five passengers riding on a DC-3. The front rows of seats were filled with stacks of Chinese and Malay-language newspapers and magazines, while the rear seats were piled high with bags of mail. We found a town barely recovered from the nearly total destruction of World War II. There were long blocks of rough wood shop buildings, open fronted on the ground floor, with family quarters above on the second floor. Most goods for sale in the shops came by sea from ships passing between Hong Kong and Singapore. Merchandise was limited in choice, quality, and prices. The shops and houses were generally lighted by kerosene-burning pressure lamps. The two hotels, like most of the shops, were Chinese managed. The hotels, most government offices, and a few commercial buildings, mostly European owned, which were of more permanent construction, were lighted by a temperamental government power-generating system. Traffic was light, roads were bad and paved only within the limited space of the central town area. For the predominant town population of Chinese, with some Malays, a few Indians and natives, such as Dusun, Bajau, and Murut, and a handful of British and

---

[8] In the village of Baginda in 1962–1963 there were 174 school aged children in a population of 751 persons. There were vernacular primary schools located 2½ and 1¼ miles from the village; one school at Bingkor was founded in 1924. The other was built in 1959 to meet the needs of the people being resettled in the Baginda development scheme. These schools were attended by 23 to 42 children; of this number 27 were boys and 15 were girls. There were 19 children who regularly attended school. There were eight village children (six boys, two girls) in a mission boarding school in Keningau, approximately 9 miles from Baginda.

Australian government officers, life was slow and not too vexing. Visitors from overseas were a rarity, since there were few passengers on the infrequent ships. Few persons appeared to possess the determination to get by air to Jesselton from Singapore.

In the interior areas of the country the pace of life was even slower. There was a once-a-week flight from the Jesselton airport to the government station of Keningau, aboard a very old fabric-covered aircraft. A narrow-gauged rail line, with wood-burning locomotives, ran down the coast from Jesselton to Beaufort, then up through the wild gorge of the rushing Padas River, ending at Melalap. To travel by road from Tenom near Melalap north to Keningau, it was necessary to take a Land-Rover-type vehicle over a muddy, one-way mountain track. The government station at Keningau consisted of the British resident officer quarters and offices; a very small police station and a police barracks; a cottage hospital and quarters for the British doctor, his family, and a British nurse; a wooden framed "rest house" for transient government officers; and some small wooden houses for junior government employees. Nearby there was a small vernacular-language primary school with some teacher's quarters. Beyond the school there was a square surrounded on three sides by new wooden shop houses of the type common to Jesselton. The goods of the Chinese merchants were the same as those sold in Jesselton. Government offices and some houses were lighted by an infrequently operating generating station. Most of the population at the post used kerosene pressure lamps. Mail service was dependent upon the train to Tenom and the condition of the road to Keningau. Some weeks no mail would arrive when the train could not run because of washouts, landslides, or fallen trees, or because the road from Tenom was impassible. Then mail would be delivered in a soggy mass of letters and broken parcels. Mail sacks were carried in the open two-wheel untilty trailer pulled along behind the four-wheel-drive vehicles. Since the trailers were also used to haul fuel, canned goods, and everything else sold in the shops of Keningau, mail sacks often were damaged. Communication with Jesselton was by means of a radio telephone link which often was inoperative. During periods of heavy rains, when floods were frequent, Keningau was totally isolated from the outside world for days at a time.

Beyond the area of the government station at Keningau, life moved at an even slower pace; the greater the distance one traveled from the station, the further one moved into the traditional life of the country. Fifty miles beyond Keningau, life was very little affected by the goods, services, and conveniences of the outside world. Here, native peoples, both Dusun and Murut, lived out their lives with relatively little reference to events of the modern world.

Then, in a quickening tempo of rising political expectations, and with a rapidly increasing volume of trade and the development of new transportation facilities, such as a new airport terminal at Jesselton, improved grass airstrips at outlying airfields, and new shipping and customs facilities, life in North Borneo began to change profoundly. When we left the country in 1960, there were few signs of the changes to come; there were no political parties, very little new permanent building, and only vague talk of improving transport and communications. We returned in 1962 to find a very different country.

There were increasingly more frequent direct flights between North Borneo and Singapore, as well as new service to Manila and Hong Kong, busy shipping schedules, a marked change in postal and hotel services, and a building boom. Capital investment by the British and by Chinese bankers and industrialists from other areas of Southeast Asia and Hong Kong had opened the country to a flow of consumer goods and made it much more accessible, to the point where by early 1963 it seemed logical to local political figures to be discussing the independence of North Borneo from Britain as part of a federation of states to include Sarawak and Brunei on the island of Borneo, Singapore, and the federated Malay states.

A rebellion in Brunei and North Borneo in December 1962, supported by the Sukarno government of Indonesia and the local Chinese Communists, provided impetus to political and economic changes already in progress. Because of the rebellion Britain moved in troops, equipment, and new administrators to cope with the threat to her control. New capital investment followed the protective forces into the country. In September 1963, North Borneo became the State of Sabah in the new nation of Malaysia, which also included at that time Sarawak, Singapore, and the Federation of Malaya. Between September 1963 and August 1966 there were frequent armed clashes along the borders of Sabah and Kalimantan (or Indonesian Borneo) between Indonesian army troops and guerrillas on one side and forces put into the field by the British on the other.

This armed "confrontation" created instability in the country's political life, but energized the economic boom because projects of strategic value were built all over the country; airfields, roads, bridges, and telephone and radio networks were improved considerably. By the time the open fighting was halted in late 1966, Sabah was a markedly different country than it had been seven years before.

Dusun society and culture changed markedly with the events of these years. Hardly a Dusun individual has been left isolated, for the population was numbered, identified, counted, and indexed by census takers, police, and military intelligence agents. Identity cards, work permits, tax cards, and all the other papers common to a modern country at war came into use. Dusun were drafted into the country's police and constabulary forces, sent to Malaya for army training and duty, put through schools to learn to repair engines, radio, and aircraft, taught to run railroad stock, radio stations, printing presses, and hired to drive buses, taxis, and road transport. Few Dusun villages were without transistor, battery-powered radios, given by the government to speed the dissemination of news and official views. By the end of 1967, in a span of less than one decade, the Dusun world had forever changed. Traditional Dusun ways still exist in many isolated Dusun communities, but even these villages no longer are really isolated. Many of the village children have gone out of the area and stayed out to learn new skills and take on new ways, opportunities, and challenges. The adults left behind are greatly unsettled by the quick pace of change and are hard put to adjust to being citizens of a state whose boundaries and national interests extend across 1000 miles of island lands and seas. A decade is a very brief time to have come to grips with the full meaning of the implications of being a member of a minority political group in one's own land. Economic power is held generally by the Chinese community in Sabah. Political power in Sabah has passed from the British into the hands of the Malays and to

Chinese operating through a few individuals selected from the local native societies. Dusun now find themselves able to hold a political franchise only when they can demonstrate that they read and write another language; they can travel only with documents issued by state and national government and are caught tightly in a rising spiral of inflationary values.

The Dusun world is undergoing profound change. It is likely that another decade, or less, will see the disappearance of some, or even many of the traditional enculturation practices I describe in the next chapters. The events of the recent past are bound to have consequences, even in so conservative an area of culture as enculturation. To understand the changes to come, it is vital that we know of the traditional Dusun enculturation process. The next chapters describe and summarize those traditional ways of enculturation. In the last chapter I will discuss some of the changes taking place.

2 / Methods of study

A N ACCOUNT OF THE METHODS USED in a study insures that other scholars can seek to restudy the same phenomena and provides some basis for an estimate of the validity of the results. I have published an account of the general methods used in study of the major configurations of traditional Dusun culture and society (Williams 1967). That text recounts the ways I chose communities to study, went about setting up my residence, began my fieldwork, and conducted interviews about and observations of Dusun culture and society.[1] In this chapter I will discuss briefly the specific methods I used in studying Dusun enculturation.

GENERAL METHODS OF RESEARCH

Anthropological studies of culture generally use the method of careful observation and interview of well-identified individuals in specified cultural and social environments. The essential ingredients of this general method of cultural anthropological research involve, (1) long-term residence, usually more than a year, in one or more local communities of a society; (2) learning the local language and then using it regularly in the course of observation and interviews with informants; (3) identification of the important, as well as the "nonimportant," social statuses (for example, hunter, potter, farmer, priest, political leader, "village loafer," "drunkard,") and the ideal and real roles of behavior associated with them, especially those based on age, sex, specialized knowledge or skills, political and economic power; (4) the careful observation and interviewing of persons holding these statuses and behaving in ways associated with them; and (5) the use of a clearly defined sample of the population as the basis for the study.

My study of Dusun enculturation began with use of this general method of research. I resided for two years in two different Dusun communities. I learned and used the Dusun language in the course of observing and interviewing Dusun about their beliefs and behavior. I made a check upon my knowledge of and skills in the language by using Dusun field assistants, acting as interpreters and translators. I systematically set about identifying the statuses common in Dusun society and made detailed records from my observations of the ways persons well known to me

---

[1] Contrasting styles of field methods used by anthropologists can be found in Beattie (1965) and Powdermaker (1966).

behaved in these statuses. I also interviewed these persons concerning their role behavior forms when occupying particular statuses. From this interviewing and observation I was able to contrast the ways Dusun acted with the ways they said they should, would, or could not behave. I also made detailed special studies of the key statuses in Dusun society, such as political and economic leader, ritual specialist, farmer, hunter and metalworker, parent, aged, and adolescent. I undertook a rigorous and full daily schedule of observing and interviewing particular people well known to me. My special subjects of regular observation and interview were drawn from a selected sample of the populations of the two communities in which we studied. I designated the households closest to our residences as the *primary social units* for our research.[2] Five other areas of the two communities were designated as *secondary social units* for observation and interviewing. Selected nearby villages were assigned to the classification of *tertiary social units*.

The primary social units in Sensuron and Baginda comprised 23 nuclear family households with a total population of 116 persons; in Sensuron, 15 households with 40 adults and 31 children were the primary social unit. In Baginda, 8 households with 19 adults and 26 children made up the primary social unit.

The five secondary social units in the two communities had a total population of 117 adults and 58 children in 38 nuclear family households. A population of approximately six hundred adults and children in 32 villages near Sensuron and Baginda comprised the tertiary social units of study.[3]

We lived for two years no more than 30 yards away from the furthest household of the two primary social units. In Sensuron we had households 15, 23, and 31 feet from the side walls of our house. Our neighbors could watch and hear us. We could observe them as easily. Very little occurred in the 23 households of the two primary social units that we did not actually see, hear, or get told about quickly. We were constantly in and about the houses of the two primary social units, talking, observing, making notes, photographs, or tape recordings or just visiting our neighbors. And our neighbors visited us regularly, for first aid, to listen to our battery-powered radio, to ask questions about our ways and beliefs, and to pass the time of day until going to or coming from work in the fields, while waiting for a rain shower to move on, and while making or repairing small tools.

We used the secondary social units to check the validity of the information gathered in our primary social units. We learned about variations of culture within a community in this manner, identified persons really key to the functioning of the

---

[2] This term and the concept was borrowed from the field guide for the study of socialization used by the Whitings (cf., J. W. M. Whiting, and others, 1966) in their studies of the enculturation processes of six cultures.

[3] Near Sensuron the tertiary social units were in communities of Tuntolub, Timbatuon, Pantai, Tibabar, Kintuntul, Piasau, Toboh, Bambangan, Talongan, Mangi Pangi, Patau, Keranhan, Tandulu, Megong, Papar, and Lintun (spelling and locations as rendered on "Plan 9187" and "Key Plan of Tambunan, Scale: 10 chains to the inch, #2006, Sheets 2, 3, 4, 7, 8" Jesselton: Deputy Director, Lands and Survey Department, North Borneo Government, 1955, 1957). Near Baginda the tertiary social unit communities were Bayangan, Binaong, Labak, Sanpak, Bingkor, Neidat, Tangkungon, Bunsit, Bandukan, Menansud, Liau Laut, Liau Darat, Patanah, Kapayan, Ranggun, and Paliu (spelling and locations as rendered on "Keningau Plain Soil Survey Map, Department of Agriculture, North Borneo Government, 1955" and on "Locality Plan of Keningau, 22–7–55, Jesselton: Deputy Director Lands and Survey Department, North Borneo Government").

community, and were able to gather basic data concerning disputes, agreements, and divisions in large-scale social units within the community. The use of secondary social units consistently focused our attention on a large sample of population in the communities we studied.

Similarly, we used the tertiary social units to determine intercommunity variations in the data we obtained in our primary and secondary social units. By enlarging our focus to a group of communities we were able to greatly extend the validity of our data.

Finally, I made a systematic effort to visit and observe and interview in Dusun communities in all other areas of Sabah which I could travel to by road or boat and on foot. After we had lived in Sensuron for six months, I attempted to begin validating my observational and interview data in other regions of the country. I tried to determine by this means regional variations in Dusun culture. While my studies are incomplete at present, they do provide a rational and empirical basis for evaluating the claims of the Dusun and of others, such as visitors, missionaries, traders, regarding supposed or purported facts of variation and differences in Dusun culture. My comparative studies provided me with specific impressions and data regarding physical, cultural, and linguistic affiliation among Dusun communities and with specific knowledge of variations in Dusun culture. I gained insight into the nature of this culture by comparative ethnological travel and study. I could have obtained these insights in no other way.

In making such studies I enlarged the focus of my observations and interviewing to the full scope of the Dusun culture. While it is quite true that no one observer can possibly comprehend every one of the culture items or traits of a society of more than 145,000 persons, it is possible, through comparative studies, which can only proceed from specific knowledge gained in intensive observation and interview of well-identified persons in a set of primary and secondary social units, to learn of the appearance and "flavor," or, in technical terms, the *eidos* and *ethos,* of a culture and society (Kroeber 1948:293) so that you know the major parts unexplored, the likely size of unexplored areas, and, most importantly, how the yet unknown aspects of culture and society may fit with the things you have already studied in great detail (Mead 1963b:604).

It is not possible to generalize, in a scientifically meaningful way, from a small primary social unit to an entire society without first undertaking systematic comparative studies in secondary social units within the community of residence, between the community of residence and other local communities, and then, finally, by travel to and comparative study in all other major units and regions of a society and culture. The study reported here is specifically accurate in detail for the primary and secondary social units of two Dusun communities, accurate in most details for the tertiary social units of the study, and, I believe, generally accurate for traditional Dusun culture.

Further comparative studies of enculturation in Dusun society will quite likely enable me to further refine and document this estimate, but the readers of this report can know that my descriptions of the Dusun enculturation process in the sample units (2 primary social units, 5 secondary social units, 32 tertiary social units) plus regular and systematic comparative travel to and study in all major regions of the Dusun society provide for a systematic sampling of Dusun life which can be extended by other scholars. Since it is very important to understand the probable applicability of statements made in this study on the basis of direct observation to Dusun groups I did not observe directly, I will discuss the problem of defining "Dusun" further.

I wish to make it clear that when I refer to "the Dusun," or use the term "Dusun" as a prefix to the concepts of culture or society, I am referring, in specific order, to data I have collected in (1) the primary social units of research, (2) the secondary social units of research, (3) the tertiary social units of research, and (4) from systematic comparative research in a quite viable society, still possessed of a coherent and dynamically functioning culture which can be and is widely designated by anthropologists through use of the conventional term "Dusun" (see Murdock 1954, 1967:26; *Ethnology,* I, 398; V, 447). The term "Dusun" is widely believed to have been applied to this population some time in the past by Malay seafaring peoples, for in modern colloquial Malay, it means "orchard" (Winstedt 1958:234) and can more formally mean "rural settlement" or "hamlet" or "inhabited patch or cultivated land" (Wilkinson 1943:292). The expression, *orang dusun* (or *pĕndusun*) in Malay is a common euphemism for "country people" or "aborigines" (Wilkinson 1943:293). Sometimes the term means "an orchard with a homestead" (Winstedt 1958:234). Since the term is so common in Malay, it has been accepted without too much question by many travelers, traders, missionaries, government officials, and some writers that the Malay peoples, on first arrival in northern Borneo, found a society living principally by farming and gardening (see Evans 1922:35) and called them by the generic name of *dusun.* There are Dusun terms, such as the verb form *mĕmĕduso,* which means "to murder," "to kill a human" in some dialects of the Dusun language, and particularly in the coastal dialects of the Penampang and Papar districts (Antonissen 1958:191; Gossens 1924; Staal 1926). The verb *mĕmĕ* denotes "to make," "to do," "to act," "to undertake." The term *duso* can mean "mankind" or "human being."[4] It is possible that the term *duso* as the native term for "mankind" could have been borrowed by the Malay peoples visiting the coastal area and adapted through simple linguistic shifts to the Malay *dusun,* and then reapplied to local peoples by the Malay speakers. It is also possible that the coastal people now called Dusun borrowed the term *dusun* from Malay speakers and adapted it by linguistic shifts to their own uses, so that it became *duso.* This is less likely than the previous hypothesis, simply because the basic term for "mankind," or "human being" in a language is not very likely to be easily altered through sporadic contacts with a trading and slave-raiding people. In addition, since the Malay Sea peoples and the Dusun both speak languages belonging to the Austronesian stock, it is possible that the terms *dusun, duso,* and so forth are contained in both languages, retaining a very old set of meanings which still find

---

[4] In Sensuron and Baginda the term *tolun* means "person" or "man." This term is also used in other Dusun dialects including those termed as *Kimanis, Tempasuk, Tuaran, Tambunan, Putatan, Tegas,* and *Ida'an.* It is cognate in these communities and dialects with the term *duso,* as in Malay, for instance, the term *orang* ("person," "man") is cognate with the term *manusia* ("mankind"). The Sama Laut Bajau term for "mankind" is *mundusia.*

expression in both groups. There is no evidence at present that this is so, but this does not rule out yet other explanations for the origin of the term "Dusun."

This should illustrate the care needed in making statements about the culture history of peoples in an area with few written records and where systematic study of culture and society is only beginning. The approximately 30,000 square miles of Sabah is fragmented by natural barriers, such as mountains, rivers, and the rain forest, into a series of localities. In times of peace, these barriers are not sufficient to impede travel and communication, although movement on foot or by boat takes effort. In a state of chronic warfare between villages and social groups seeking to keep their fortunes in balance these natural barriers could assume some meaning in leading to different degrees of social and cultural isolation.

The first Europeans to come to northern Borneo perpetuated a myth that there were vast differences among peoples native to the area. This myth was a very effective device for maintaining political control with little use of power and was used by the North Borneo Chartered Company throughout its control of the country. The native peoples were told repeatedly that there were such great differences between them that it was best to allow the Europeans to negotiate and adjudicate matters between villages and areas. Since few Europeans could speak the local languages but could speak some Malay and some natives could speak Malay, from long contact with Malay traders, and some Malay traders had learned local languages in Borneo, the North Borneo Chartered Company introduced Malay as the "official" government language. Malay also became the language of the "vernacular" schooling supported by the North Borneo Chartered Company. This tended to provide strong support for the rationale by the government that the native peoples were so different from each other that a common language had to be found for them to communicate.

The fact today is that Dusun from Tambunan, in the interior of Sabah, have no basic difficulty speaking to, understanding, being understood, and interacting socially and culturally with Dusun from other areas of Sabah, including the Tuaran, Penampang, Kinarut, Papar, Membakut, Keningau, Ranau, Labuk, Kudat, and Kinabatangan regions. There is a genuine sharing of linguistic, social, and cultural comprehension among Dusun from these major regions of Sabah. This fact is recognized by the Dusun and was noted by the British Government commission, which set forth the plan for inclusion of Sabah in Malaysia (Cobbold Commission, 1962) and recognized by some British Colonial officials long resident in the country (see Jones 1962:47). In the face of this fact, it seems in error to argue that the natural (but traversable) barriers which divided Sabah into regions produced, even in times of chronic warfare, basic differences in peoples native to the country which today result in every village being a unique social unit.

This does not mean that there are not variations in social and cultural forms between Dusun villages within a region and in different regions. There are variations, particularly at the level of cultural analysis, termed "items," "traits," and "trait complexes." At the higher level of abstraction of data from social and cultural behavior, such as patterns, configurations, values, and themes, the amount and types of variation sharply decreases. Whether you see great variations in Sabah among the Dusun depends on the factors of your experience through training and long-term residence, and then systematic comparative studies, and whether you choose to emphasize low-level data of abstraction showing differences or higher level abstractions of data showing similarities.

If you take an example from the American society, the problem is easier to visualize. I say that I carry my groceries in a sack. Other Americans speak of toting their vittles in a poke. Still others say they heist their food in a bag. These dialect variations do not prove that there are three separate cultures in the United States. You could argue to this effect, but few Americans would bother with the statement, for it ignores the fact that we tend to secure our major subsistence from a central location. That pattern of behavior is more important analytically and theoretically in the study of American culture than the dialect differences, for the patterned behaviors shared by a people are a true test of their belonging to one culture and one society.

In Dusun life, if you compare the discrete explanations for sterility in marriage (see Chapter 3), there will be several minor variations in the natural regions of Sabah of one general belief, that the husband's and wife's "blood" will not come together to conceive a child. The responses of Dusun informants from different regions do vary concerning some detail of the reasons for sterility, but wherever you travel in Sabah to Dusun villages, sterility is viewed as very serious, since the matter involves broad Dusun conceptions and patterns of an adult's social relations and property and a basic definition of adulthood. It would be easy to say that there are variations in responses, while ignoring the patterns of value implicit and present in beliefs about sterility. This depends, however, on whether you want to treat every village as quite unique and therefore a special case for study, or whether you seek to discern the patterns, configurations, values, and themes which a functioning society and culture possess. I have chosen to treat Dusun culture as a functioning, dynamic reality, observable, understandable, and admitting of abstract analysis.

SPECIFIC METHODS OF RESEARCH

In addition to the general method of cultural anthropological research I used quite specific methods in gaining data of Dusun enculturation. When I went to the field I carried copies of professional articles and texts which had special statements about research on enculturation processes. I had copies of many of the previous studies of enculturation in other societies (for example, Du Bois 1944; Sears, Maccoby, and Levin 1957; Mead 1928a, 1930b, 1937, 1949, 1956; Bateson and Mead 1942; Dennis 1940; Spiro 1958) and journal articles (Mead 1928b, 1930a, 1931, 1932, 1939–1940, 1940, 1946, 1947, 1952, 1953, 1954a, b), which I reread in the field as I did my work, for theoretical and methodological clues as to my best procedure in research. I also had copies of texts and articles concerned with the topic of the relation between culture and personality (for example, Hsu 1954; Honigmann 1954; Haring 1956; Henry 1958; Kluckhohn 1954; Kluckhohn, Murray, and Schneider 1953; Sargent and Smith 1949).

I also had a mimeographed copy of a then unpublished "field guide for the study of socialization," which had most graciously been provided me by John Whiting. This guide was used by the members of teams of scholars making studies in the mid-1950s in six different cultures under the directions of John and Bernice Whiting, Irvin L. Child, William W. Lambert, and others. The field guide since has been published in a revised form (Whiting et al. 1966). Although I have reservations concerning some of the theoretical and conceptual assumptions and analytic systems on which the field guide is based, I did use it regularly in the course of my research on Dusun enculturation. Therefore, although I worked completely independently and with some different theoretical orientations (see Williams 1958) than the six teams supervised by the Whitings and others, my study of Dusun enculturation should be considered related to the publications which have derived from the Whiting six-cultures studies (see Fischer and Fischer 1966; LeVine and LeVine 1966; Maretzki and Maretzki 1966; Minturn and Hitchcock 1966; Nydegger and Nydegger 1966; and Romney and Romney 1966).

These studies all began with the general method of cultural anthropological research and broadly followed the special procedures for study of the enculturation process in whole and functioning societies. The major differences between my research and that carried on by the Whiting teams are: (1) I spent more time in the field in the course of my study and so was able to make a more detailed study of the ways the enculturation process functioned in the context of Dusun culture; (2) I was able to employ a greater variety of methods (see later discussion) in my research since I was not working as a member of a team organized to secure specific kinds of enculturation data to validate particular types of hypotheses about the relations between child-training practices and personality systems; and (3) while I approached the data of Dusun enculturation knowledgable about and not unsympathetic to the particular theoretical conceptions of learning and behavior employed in the studies of Whiting and his associates, I could and did draw upon a broad range of ideas about human learning in seeking data of Dusun enculturation.

These differences enabled me to see a variety of data and remain alert for new enculturation clues and suggestions which I might not have attended to or perceived in Dusun life had I been working within the boundaries of special theoretical and methodological considerations. There is no question, however, that my methodological sophistication in the study of enculturation was considerably enhanced by my access to and use of the field guide of Whiting and his associates for the study of socialization.

In the second year of research on Dusun enculturation I also used a field guide for the "study of child life" which was prepared by Sister Inez Hilger from her studies of enculturation in Chippewa, Arapaho, and Araucanian cultures (Hilger 1960). I found this guide a quite valuable source for leads in interviewing on various enculturation topics, rechecking materials already obtained, and in ordering data of observation and interview.[5]

---

[5] The Hilger field guide extends considerably the topics for enculturation interview and observation suggested in the *Outline of Cultural Materials* by Murdock et al. (1961). I also used the field guide of Murdock et al., but primarily in my work on other configurations of Dusun culture.

In addition, I used regularly six research methods in my study of Dusun enculturation that have been employed productively in other field studies of the causal relations between particular events in enculturation (such as feeding) and particular types of adult behavior (dependent behavior and so forth). These methods, which are described in detail by Barnouw (1963) and Honigmann (1954, 1967) are:

1. Sampling by use of oral questionnaires;
2. Studies of family interactions (father-oldest son; mother-oldest son, and so forth);
3. Life-history collection and analysis;
4. Dream, vision, and phantasy collection and analysis;
5. Cultural product analysis (such as folklore, art, music);
6. Projective tests, including the Rorschach, modified Thematic Apperception Test, Machover Draw-A-Person Test, and Lowenfeld Mosaic Test.

Each of these specific methods is productive of limited amounts of enculturation data. These methods often have to be adapted to the local cultural situation (written questionnaires cannot be used in a nonliterate society), as was the instance in my Dusun research.[6] Generally these data are more useful in providing insight into the psychological consequences of enculturation practices in a society than in revealing the patterned nature of specific enculturation techniques. Honigmann (1967: 206–209) recently has reviewed and discussed the special methodology of study of enculturation.[7]

I also used three quite special methods of study to try to seek out the several patterns of enculturation used in Dusun culture and to learn of the specific details of culture traits and trait complexes which comprise each enculturation pattern. These three special methods are (1) chronological sequence records, (2) behavior schedule records, and (3) play records.

In limited social settings, such as a primary social unit of observation and interview, records of specific acts can be made for later analysis; thus, a mother is observed as she breast feeds a newborn, a father as he punishes his youngest son, or a grandmother as she works at drying rice with the assistance of her son's younger daughters. Such records, made in notebooks and using cameras and sometimes tape recorders, note the context of the time of beginning and ending of the acts, the

---

[6] For specific examples and discussions of these methods see D. Eggan (1949, 1952), Hallowell (1947), Barnouw (1949), C. Kluckhohn (1954), Blumer (1939), Dollard (1935), G. Allport (1942), A. Leighton and D. Leighton (1949), Aberle (1951), Lewis (1959, 1961, 1966), Heyer (1953), Lantis (1953), Hsu (1953), Wallace (1950), Barry (1957), Henry and Henry (1944), Landy (1960), Ritchie (1957), and Roheim (1941).

[7] Some comments on the methods needed for study of enculturation (see Minturn and Lambert, 1964:292) have proceeded from a focus on the cultural context of enculturation to specifying a variety of kinds of special social and cultural data which are proposed as being vital to understanding this process. It should be noted that these requirements for special data very often follow from the conceptions of cause and effect links between enculturation and adult character and the way research hypotheses have been defined and are not necessarily requisite for understanding enculturation in each human society. Fieldworkers should gather all data possible during their research, but they must not allow their work to be shaped by rigid schedules of data to be secured.

physical setting, the persons present, and those taking part. In a year's collection of such chronological sequence records it is possible to compile hundreds of distinct and discrete accounts of particular and limited enculturation events. In my Dusun study, I was able to discern from these records that although Dusun parents could easily account in interviews for five classes of physical punishment with ten distinct acts, which were ranked as more severe to less severe as punishments (see Chapter 5), only 29 of more than 350 separate instances we observed of adults punishing children were of the kind termed by adults as "very severe" in nature. While Dusun parents talked about how harsh they were in punishing children, in fact the chronological sequence records demonstrated that in only 8 percent of all punishment acts recorded were the actions of a nature said to be harsh.

Totaled in the hundreds of hours, chronological sequence records comprise data providing for ways of determining the broad activities of specific enculturation patterns and suggest some functional links between patterns of enculturation and may give evidence of levels of cultural complexity, as for instance in the ways in which Dusun ideally say one thing about physical punishment of children, yet obviously act quite to the contrary.[8]

The behavior schedule method consists of a precise accounting of the activities of a number of key individuals, both adults and children, selected carefully by age, sex, status, and power position in the community through a particular calendar period, such as a day, week, month, or a group of months. This method is effectively illustrated in the work of Geddes (1954) among the Land Dayak of Borneo and is based upon the development of a similar procedure for research with children by Barker and Barker (1961) by Barker and Wright (1951, 1955). The behavior schedule record is a means of accounting exactly for the time spent by particular individuals in different types of activities over a finite period which is of considerably longer duration than is involved in making chronological sequence records. Also, the focus of concern in the making of behavior schedule records is upon the individual behaving as an individual in particular types of patterned acts rather than being primarily concerned with specific interactions, or transactions, between individuals, as in chronological sequence records.

This method has been generally discussed and also used extensively in enculturation studies by Barker and Barker (1961), Henry (1960), Wolfenstein (1955), and Heyns and Lippitt (1954) and was a principal method used by the Whiting six-culture study teams (Whiting, *et al.* 1966:39–118).

Behavior schedule records demonstrate that Dusun children engage in many different types of activities (see Chapter 5) from infancy to adolescence. These records also point to significant alterations in child care in the period between two and five years of age. These records further make clear that adolescent Dusun in the two primary social units studied spent less than 20 percent of their time in a calendar year engaged in work tasks, despite the ideal statements of both parents and children that "children always help their parents work."

---

[8] Margaret Mead, working with Gregory Bateson (1942) and Francis MacGregor (1951), has produced two substantive and very important examples of enculturation study using in part the chronological-sequence method of study.

This method demands one or more additional observers working at the tasks of making records and so is very demanding and expensive to use (see comments in Whiting, *et al.* 1966:107–109). It is a method difficult to master, but it is a key procedure in study of enculturation processes.

The method of making play records consists essentially in providing children with a defined area and toys for play and then making detailed chronological sequence records to note the sequence and patterned activities in play. I used areas adjacent to our residence in both Sensuron and Baginda for play situations. I regularly made these areas available to younger children and provided them with local materials (bamboo, stones, rattan, vine, and the like) as well as with toys purchased in nearby trading centers, such as Tambunan and Keningau, and toys brought specially from the United States (dolls, animals, balls, blocks) to enable the children to play in a spontaneous manner. I recorded conversations and social interactions and I often interviewed younger children as they played.

I learned a great deal about Dusun "child culture" in this manner. I also learned about ideal dimensions of Dusun enculturation as well as discovering the ways more perceptive and insightful children noted the differences between the things adults said and the ways they behaved. The essentially unsophisticated and vulnerable child perception of the Dusun world was valuable in constructing an abstract model of the total enculturation process. This method is very time consuming also and demands patience of a high order.

The use of the general method of cultural anthropological study and of the other methods of study of enculturation processes has produced a body of data, in the form of written records, films, and tape recordings, which makes possible the writing of a text such as this one. I have gathered a substantial amount of material, far more than can be incorporated into a volume of limited size, which clearly indicates the major forms and meanings and many of the functions of Dusun enculturation patterns. In the pages which follow I use several varieties of styles of reporting to describe these patterns of enculturation. In many instances I set down highly abstracted and generalized statements about an aspect of the enculturation process ("A mother spends most of her time in the first month and much of her time in the first six months after birth caring for an infant"—Chapter 4) that are derived directly from behavior and chronological-sequence records, and the general method of observation and interviewing. I also quote directly from individuals to illustrate the content or dimensions of a particular real or ideal enculturation belief or act, and I have included some brief excerpts from my actual field notes, as records of limited, direct observation of an event (see Chapter 5, the section "Physical Punishment in Childhood"). I have tried to balance these forms of reporting in this brief text. Because of space limitations I have not been able to provide extensive examples of questionnaires and data from other research methods used in our studies.

A COMMENT ON METHODS OF ENCULTURATION STUDY

It is clear that special methods of research in enculturation must follow from and are dependent upon the general method of cultural anthropological research. As the general method of research is refined and extended, the special methods of study will benefit. It is equally clear that much remains to be done in the development of special methods of enculturation research. Fieldworkers will have to remain constantly alert to the development of new procedures and techniques of research in anthropology, psychology, sociology, and other social science fields to be able to devise more efficient and comprehensive means of obtaining, classifying, and summarizing data of enculturation. New technology in the form of portable equipment designed to handle large amounts of complex data may add considerably to our ability to conduct meaningful research on enculturation. In turn, this may add to our ability to undertake more productive studies of socialization.

3 / Conception, pregnancy, and birth

CONVENTIONAL DUSUN BELIEF about and behavior in conception, pregnancy, and birth is described in this chapter. These beliefs and behavior provide a distinct setting within which subsequent enculturation of the child takes place. Knowing the details of beliefs and practices used in conception, pregnancy, and childbirth provides insight into the ways the Dusun or any other people value a child, view its development, and prepare for the social adjustments necessary at birth.

CONCEPTION

Dusun believe that conception occurs as the consequence of the hot blood of the female and male mixing during intercourse. The explanation of conception generally used is that during a time of sexual excitement, the blood of the female and male heat progressively and tend to concentrate in the sexual anatomy. Semen is considered a special type of hot blood and as absolutely necessary to conception.

The Dusun concept of paternity is that while men and women are equally responsible for care of a child, the male "begins" the process of pregnancy by discharge of "special hot blood" during an orgasm in intercourse. Fines and penalties for illegitimacy are more severe for fathers than mothers, and during light teasing between husbands and wives, men often say, "Do not be cruel, because I can make the child." A woman will object to her husband beating an older child with the stylized expression, "Do not be so diligent in beating that child you made!"

A woman having intercourse is supposed to have her blood concentrate in her abdomen, where it becomes hotter and hotter until the point is reached where the boiling blood turns to steam. At this point, which is believed to be signaled by a female orgasm, fetal growth is said to commence. The mother's steamlike drops of blood congeal in the womb with the semen of the father to create the fetus. It is believed that the mother's blood continues to boil during pregnancy if she regularly has intercourse. Fetal growth is explained as the process in which drops of hot blood congeal onto the growing child. In the first months the fetus is considered to be the size of the tip of a little finger, growing at two months to the diameter of the tip of a woman's big toe and at three months to the diameter of a woman's forearm. The process of fetal growth is believed to involve the addition of hot blood

34

drops to each dimension of the child, so that it grows continually all around. Intercourse is said to be continued regularly, at least once a week, from determination of pregnancy until the end of the seventh month after menses cease. Intercourse is considered vital to the process of continued fetal development and a "normal" pregnancy. The heating of the female's blood by orgasm and the addition of the male semen is felt necessary to continued development of the child. After the third month the fetus is supposed to suck his thumb to gather more hot blood for his growth. This thumb sucking process is also believed training for nursing after birth.

An inability to conceive is treated by Dusun as a serious matter since it involves the parent's social relations, property, and kinship obligations and especially the definition of adulthood. The general explanation for sterility is contained in the statement "Their blood will not come together." Usually it is considered to be a woman's fault in failure of a married couple to conceive, although occasionally village gossip will indicate that both husband and wife are considered such "bad people" that they are barren because they are not fit to be parents. Some sterility is recognized, or explained, as the consequence of damage, through accidents, to male genitals. Except for old men, impotence in the sexual act is claimed unknown among Dusun males, and is not considered as a cause of sterility. In a few instances sterility is explained as the consequence of a "disease giver" spirit (called *tàmpuàn*) having intercourse with a wife or husband while they sleep and causing them to become barren.

A barren Dusun women seeks out the cause of her inability to conceive in a series of divinations involving "touching" rituals by a female ritual specialist. In the course of the divination, the ritual specialist palpates the womb to see if it is "right." If the womb is felt to be tilted in an "improper" position, a special ritual is held to correct it. This ritual, termed "to make it right," is said to involve "putting the womb back in the middle of the belly." Women are also felt to be barren because their womb is "stuck to the backbone." A medicinal potion (*tàtàpes*) is applied by a female ritual specialist to the lower back of the afflicted woman. The substance is covered with a cloth bound about the body, to try to effect a cure known as "unsticking the womb from the backbone." Sterility caused by the *tàmpuàn* usually is divined by a female ritual specialist, and a cure is attempted in a ritual involving the offering of a pig to the disease giver as appeasement.

There are several social consequences of sterility. Since they have no children, a couple are not considered adults, despite their chronological ages and obvious skills and knowledge. Relatives of the couple are embarrassed by the sterility, and neighbors have difficulty dealing with the couple on the same basis as they would if the couple had children. The usual social consequences of long-term sterility are desertion of the wife by her husband or a divorce blaming the wife for the couple's barrenness. At the end of seven years a childless marriage may be dissolved by simple mutual agreement between the husband and wife. If a childless couple are viewed by their neighbors and friends and relatives as being possessed of all the ideal characteristics of parents, they will be urged to adopt orphaned or illegitimate children to maintain the marriage.

A woman will seek to induce conception by frequent intercourse with her husband. She will also try to eat foods she has a special fondness for and begin to avoid certain locations, animals, and foods. The food cravings are considered vital to cure of sterility, since their satisfaction causes the blood to become ready for conception. A woman will avoid or exhibit an aversion to foods she thinks bad for the blood. She will not eat certain jungle products, such as the bananalike fruit of a particular jungle plant, and she may choose a common food such as sweet potatoes, pork, or some fruits as being "bad" for her blood. She may stop drinking one variety of rice wine, while continuing to drink other types.

There are certain foods no woman seeking to induce conception or to maintain a pregnancy will eat: the jungle jackfruit, the meat of the pangolin, the meat of a monkey, and the meat of the red deer. The eating of the jackfruit and monkey meat are believed to lead the baby to become a thief. The eating of pangolin (scaly anteater) meat will cause a fetus to ball up and grow like the animal. The eating of the meat of the red deer is believed to lead to uterine bleeding during pregnancy. Since the red deer appears at certain locations in the jungle regularly, as a woman also menstruates regularly, the eating of red deer will lead to periodic bleeding. A woman seeking to conceive may walk around some location in the village she has chosen as potentially harmful to her conception. She may avoid quarrelsome neighbors to preclude the effects of their "bad words" or anger on her blood. She may cover her eyes at the sight of a tortoise or her ears at the call of the jungle owl to avoid harm to her abilities to conceive. The sweet meat of the deer called *paus* may be refused by a woman seeking to conceive, because the word *paus* sounds like *komous,* or "offended," and she wishes not to offend any supernatural being who might try to harm her conception. If a barren woman can "feel" none of these desires and aversions, it is believed necessary and proper for her husband to take her place. In the course of trying to bring about his wife's conception, the husband will undergo the food cravings and aversions his wife would normally experience. Meanwhile, the wife proceeds with her normal daily routine. The common explanation for a wife's inability to "feel" the desires and aversions is that while in her mother's womb, she did not like the special foods and practices that led to her conception. A man who wants to take his wife's place is felt to be able to do so because while he was in his mother's womb he was "pleased" with the special foods and practices which led to his conception and fetal growth. The husband follows these practices during the time his wife is trying to conceive to cure her barrenness. Both husband and wife readily accept suggestions from other adults for special practices for causing conception. A man acting the part of his wife may be "too embarrassed" to have the fact known generally and may have to discreetly make inquiries as he seeks knowledge of practices to induce conception to substitute for those he is rejecting as unsuccessful.

There is no general concern with prevention of conception and there is no policy or program for population control in Dusun culture. Questions about birth control amuse Dusun adults, for whom children are vital and necessary to success in the adult world. There is no concern for preventing conception, legitimate or illegitimate, by women who are known to be "mad," "stupid," or diseased. Dusun communities may contain women who are unmarried because of their defects of body or "mind," but who have borne several children.

PREGNANCY

Dusun women judge the onset of pregnancy by a variety of physical signs. If their menses have ceased for two to three months, they then tend to judge their condition by the darkening of the areola of their nipples, abdominal protuberance, the mottling and darkening of their abdomen and breasts, and nausea and vomiting (morning sickness) associated with pregnancy. Women also claim that paleness of the face and desire for "sour" foods are positive indications of pregnancy. Once pregnancy is determined the time of delivery is forecast by counting ahead from the first missed menstrual period. A woman usually consults with her mother, mother's mother, mother's sisters, and often a female ritual specialist in judging pregnancy and forecasting time of delivery. The forecasting of delivery appears haphazard since many women claim to have carried babies for 10 and 11 months, and in some instances for a year. The usual belief about the term of pregnancy is that "it depends on the baby" with no precise specification of the full term of the condition. Some women use the markers of the annual cycle of agricultural labor to judge the progress of their pregnancy.

If a woman knows she is pregnant she works normally and is not ritually isolated. Some women avoid the carrying of heavy loads. They may avoid riding astride a water buffalo. If nausea sets in, a woman will curtail some of her tasks and rest part of each day at home, while treating herself with an application of *tàtàpes* bound across her abdomen and drinking a substance called *hàmpàn,* a liquid extract from a particular jungle creeper. Toward the end of the term of pregnancy, when abdominal protuberance is great, women tend to confine their work tasks to the household. Then they usually cook, repair tools, and prepare materials for the birth.

Pregnant women are supposed to have a variety of powerful, idiosyncratic food cravings. They are believed to crave "sour things" such as one special variety of mango, or oranges and lemons. They are supposed to intensely dislike "bitter foods" such as many varieties of the vegetables regularly gathered in the jungle. Certain meats are believed to be powerfully attractive to pregnant women (domestic pig, chicken), while others (deer, wild pig, monkey, lizard, rat) are felt repulsive and harmful. I witnessed a woman in the seventh to eighth month of pregnancy deliberately vomit a meal onto the house floor on learning that the meat she had supposed to be domestic pig was from a jungle pig shot by my assistant. Her explanation was simply, "That meat would harm the baby!"

The animals and events giving bad omens in daily life are also considered as meaningful to pregnant women.[1] An especially bad omen for a pregnant woman is the sight of a tortoise; it is feared the baby's head will pass in and out of the vagina as the tortoise's head moves in and out of its shell. Jungle owls are feared because it is believed that like the owl, the baby's head will grow too large for the body, making it impossible to deliver.

It is also believed that the same practices of food cravings and aversions followed

---

[1] See Williams (1965), Chapter 4, for a discussion of omens, luck, and chance.

in seeking to introduce conception will promote the growth and well-being of a baby during pregnancy. If a woman feels she cannot follow these practices, they can apply for the husband during pregnancy. In a total of 70 marriages in the three most recent generations in Sensuron, 10 husbands acknowledged that they had taken the place of their wives at some time during pregnancy in order to "feel" and meet the necessary desires and aversions.

In the third ascending (or grandparental) Sensuron generation, 4 of 9 husbands said they had taken on at least part of their wives' cravings and aversions during part of the first pregnancy. In the second and first ascending generations, 4 of 20 husbands and 2 of 31 husbands said they had participated in their wives' first pregnancy in this way. Only 1 of the 10 husbands claimed he had taken on "all" of his wife's cravings and desires.[2]

Dusun women believe that if they "behave well" during pregnancy, the baby will grow normally and be large, fully developed, and healthy. In addition to concern with regular intercourse, fulfilling the expected food desires and aversions, and observing common taboos on the sights and sounds of some animals and events, pregnant women are supposed to pay attention to their drinking habits. The variety of rice wine termed *àrehan* ("it turns itself") is to be avoided because it will cause the baby to turn and lead to miscarriage. Pregnant women do not often carry heavy loads.

Many pregnant women anticipate *àuenķàt,* the sickness that may come to a woman at childbirth. This affliction is believed to be carried on the rays of the morning sun, borne on certain kinds of cold breezes, and associated with "dirty places," especially those that are muddy, wet, or smoky from fires or tobacco. A pregnant woman will avoid working in or walking through muddy areas. She tends to take care not to be out too much at times of the day or on days when the *àuenķàt* may be about, and a pregnant women tries to stay out of the direct way of smoke from cooking fires, cigarettes, or the burning off of the jungle for clearing fields. Smoke is felt to be a "dirty" substance and to make a pregnant woman's blood "become cold and harden." Women in the later stages of pregnancy say they often will leave parties because of the smell of *àrehan*-type rice wine and the amount of smoke in a crowded house. In addition to anticipating a relationship between dirt and cold and *àuenķàt,* pregnant women feel that "hard" foods can lead to sickness. Some women eat no foods with a consistency defined as hard, such as certain jungle fruits and vegetables. Many pregnant women regularly take some "soft foods" such as a broth of chicken to insure that their blood will stay "soft" and continue to promote the baby's growth to a healthy and normal birth. There are no formal ritual practices associated with a "normal" pregnancy. Pregnant women are allowed to continue their work in the rice fields, under the belief that "it is good to show the rice a woman is fertile, so that it will not become ill."

Just before the uterus has descended into the pelvis, pregnant women can do

---

[2] The concept (*mèṇàbe dè tàndu*) is somewhat similar in form to that of *couvade,* a practice where at the birth of a child, the mother gets up and resumes her household duties, while the father goes to bed in her stead. The *couvade* has been reported from South America, Africa, India, and China. For a discussion see A. L. Kroeber, 1948, *Anthropology,* New York, Harcourt, pp. 542–543.

some heavy work again, since it is believed that "the baby is full grown and no harm can come to him now." However, the general rule is that in any pregnancy the customary Dusun ways should be carefully observed. It is believed especially important that a woman be "very careful" in her first pregnancy. Women who have borne a child that lived are supposed to be able "to judge their own strength" and so determine the course of behavior in pregnancy more easily than before.

Miscarriages are attributed to the mother's blood becoming "hard" and "cool" in the uterus because of her failure to observe one of the expected conventions of conception and pregnancy. The products of miscarriage are buried without ceremony by a woman's husband. Usually, these remains are disposed of in a shallow hole dug in the jungle away from the village. When the miscarriage is completed, a woman is expected to stay in her house from two to four days for *rumèdun,* "the rest after birth." There are no generally used rituals for miscarriage, although a woman in her first pregnancy may ask a female ritual specialist to try to divine the act or acts which caused the miscarriage. After the period of *rumèdun* women who have miscarried return to their normal work in the household and fields. Dusun women recognize a "miscarriage" as occurring after the fourth month of pregnancy and up to the time of lightening.

Despite the desire of Dusun to have children, abortions do occur, most often to prevent an illegitimate birth. One method of inducing abortion is for a woman to fall on her abdomen over a log or length of bamboo and then to roll over the object repeatedly. The juices of some jungle plants thought to induce abortion (for example, "hibiscus" or one of a genus of herbs, trees, or shrubs of the mallow family) are taken at the time of this or similar acts to induce abortion. The act of aborting by a women is considered as less serious than bearing an illegitimate child. An unmarried woman's relatives are relieved if she aborts, since the act avoids the unpleasant consequences of a public hearing for bearing a child without having been married. There is a generally shared feeling among the Dusun that abortion by an unmarried woman is the best solution to a potentially difficult social situation. Hence, there is no punishment meted out for the act of inducing an abortion. Married women who seek to abort are considered "mad" and treated as such, since the "normal" desire of all married women is to have as many children as possible. Spontaneous abortions are considered unfortunate events because of the desire of parents for children.

The first child is considered the parent's "greatest joy," and subsequent children are felt to be important, but secondary to the fact of the first act of parenthood. There is a general preference for male babies. Fathers do not openly brag during a wife's pregnancy for fear of causing loss of the child, but the apparent success of conception and a normal pregnancy is often more than the young father can bear to conceal. His friends may help out his desire to be a "boaster of the first child" by doing his boasting for him, while he stands by beaming at the compliments to his adulthood. Such comments are still circumspect, with little mention of the mother or baby, to avoid causing them harm. A couple's parents are publicly and visibly pleased at the prospects of being grandparents, and especially so for the first time. Many prospective first-time grandparents willingly run the risk of their reputations being damaged by openly boasting of the event of birth, because of the social significance to them of becoming members of the grandparental generation. Since the wisest persons in Dusun society are the oldest persons and since the definition of being "old" begins with the fact of being a grandparent, a little boasting and visible pride is usually forgiven in new grandparents. Brothers and sisters of a couple to be parents for the first time are prone to boast a bit too, for the status of "uncle" and "aunt" also carries the prestige of age and therefore wisdom is implied in these terms. Pregnancy sets conditions for changes in a family with other children. During the months prior to delivery, older children try out the terms they expect the new child to use in addressing them; "older brother," "older sister," and the like, are often used in play by the friends of children of a woman about to give birth.

The youngest sibling is often prepared for the birth of a child by his mother's comments concerning his approaching the time when he can move from sleeping between his parents to sleeping with his brothers and sisters by the house fire pit, and by his mother's comments about his impending freedoms of movement and play because his mother will be "busy" caring for the new baby.

BIRTH

At the time of lightening or shortly after, most pregnant women prepare for delivery of the child by making medicinal potions and readying a place in the house for the birth. A particular species of spider is collected in some quantity, then burned in a pot over a hot fire to reduce it to ashes. The spider ash is added to scrapings from the surface of the woman's fingernails and these materials are then added to a jungle vegetable, which is pounded in a stone mortar with a stone pestle as the juices of several jungle creepers are mixed into the preparation. This substance is applied to the umbilical cord and navel of the infant just after birth to "cure" it from any sickness caused by the act of birth. Women prepare food for use in case of hemorrhaging on delivery; a broth of boiled chicken, rice, and a potatolike jungle vegetable is drunk to stop uterine bleeding. A special cloth binding is prepared for tying about the body at the level of the uterus to help in staunching uterine hemorrhages.

Just before birth women usually pick up a small piece of bamboo from the litter about the house yard and carve it into a sharp-edged knife for use in cutting the umbilical cord. A new sleeping mat, of woven bamboo, is selected and laid out to dry in the sun, then placed in position in the house near the wall which is on the "upper" or uphill side. It is believed bad luck will come from delivery on the "downhill" side of the house. Souls of the dead always proceed to the land of the dead in a downhill, downriver direction and so the infant and mother are believed in peril in being oriented in such directions.

A woman about to deliver also prepares a special strap made of bark cloth. She collects the inner bark of a large jungle softwood tree which also is used in making articles of clothing, pounds it into a pliable form at a stream edge, then twists it into a rope long enough to reach from the lower house roof stringers to her upraised arms as she kneels to deliver. This strap is supposed vital to "proper" delivery since it is part of the "old ways." Women may use the heavy bark straps from large carrying baskets if delivery occurs before preparations are completed. If a woman feels it necessary to do so, she can insure an easy delivery of the infant by a simple ritual. She loops a piece of the special barkcloth strap about her abdomen, ties it tightly, then cuts it while saying, "As I cut this strap, so it will loose the baby from my belly."

At the onset of labor a woman usually sends for her mother to act as midwife in delivery. In many instances of birth a senior female ritual specialist acts as midwife, assisted by a woman's mother. If her mother is dead, and there is no ritual specialist nearby, a woman about to deliver will seek assistance from an older sister or a close female friend, providing they have borne children and are reputed "to know the work of birth." The husband is put to work building a fire, cutting a supply of wood, and carrying fresh water from the river. Often, his major task during delivery is to boil the hot water to be drunk by the mother during delivery and to be used to wash the baby and to clean the mother's body from the products of birth. Older children of a family sometimes are sent to stay with relatives, usually the father's parents, and sometimes the mother's father and mother. Children under the ages of five or six years often are allowed to remain in the house during delivery, since they are believed to have no comprehension of the act which is occurring. All other persons are generally excluded unless the midwife or mother especially requests their presence.

A woman beginning labor sits or lays out on the sleeping mat placed under the barkcloth line hanging from a house roof stringer. When the second stage of labor begins, she loops the line about both wrists and sinks back down on her calves with her knees rotated outward. If she has not prepared the line, she may kneel and hold a main wall support. The midwife kneels before her and begins a gentle massage of the abdomen to "push the baby out." Hot water is periodically passed to the midwife by the husband or one of the women present, to be drunk by the mother to facilitate easy passage of the child. While the second stage of labor proceeds, the midwife, if a ritual specialist, repeats a brief verse to insure easy delivery. If the midwife is not a ritual specialist, one may be called to repeat the ritual. The ritual verse is as follows:

I take up the secret waters, the waters to make things loose and smooth.

What do I expect in doing this?

I expect things to become loose and smooth!

I take coconut oil to rub in with the sacred waters to make them looser and smoother.

Look! Look at that!

The hair which is curled on her belly now combs and straightens nicely.

Each follows the other as I comb them out, smooth and loose.

Not even that unborn child inside the stomach will stay fitted tightly.

Look! Imagine I have a key!

I take the key, to open, to open the box that holds the baby.

The box will come open, now! and everything will be out!

And so, the unborn baby will come out easily, come out smoothly, from the womb of the mother![3]

These verses are repeated several times as the ritual specialist rubs a mixture of water and coconut oil on the abdomen of the woman in labor.

If the midwife judges the baby not to be in "good position" for birth, she uses a special massage to insure the baby is in "proper birth position." When rupture of the bag of amniotic fluid occurs, the midwife urges the mother to "push down hard" and begins to massage her abdomen in sharp downward strokes. As the child is born, the midwife holds it with one of her hands until it is fully clear of the mother while with the other hand she pushes down on the lower abdomen of the mother. Then she lays the infant across her knees, face upward, and gently massages its chest with one hand while cleaning its eyes, nostrils, and mouth of birth matter with the forefinger of the other hand. The father places a bowl of hot water by the midwife, and as she waits for the umbilical cord to stop pulsating, usually a period of five minutes or so, she cleans the infant of the *vernix caseosa*. When the cord has stopped pulsing, the midwife stretches it to the forehead of the infant, where she ties one ligature, usually made of a wild cotton thread (although commercial thread may now be used in some instances) and then ties another one an inch or so toward the placenta and cuts between them with the bamboo knife prepared by the mother. She drains the cord into the abdomen of the infant by holding it up from the belly, then ties a simple knot in its severed end with thread to prevent any "sickness" from entering the cord. The thread is then wound in a spiral around the cord down to the infant's abdomen. The cord is stretched to the nasal bridge of the female infants and as far as it will reach over the forehead of the male babies, because of belief that if a boy's cord is "cut long," he will not be "short tempered," "bad tempered," or develop into a child known as "a short cord," or "bad" boy. A girl's cord is cut shorter because "it is expected that girls will naturally be shorter tempered than boys."

As the midwife cares for the baby, the mother is given more hot water to drink and her abdomen is massaged by one of the other women present, or her husband, to assist in expulsion of a placenta in the third stage of labor. The midwife applies the "curing" potion prepared by the mother to the cord of the infant, then takes up the end of the thread which has been spiral-wrapped about the cord and ties the cord off with a ligature about 2 to 3 inches from the baby's abdomen, coils it on

---

[3] This is a "free translation" from the Dusun language. I transcribed these verses by use of a tape recorder, then asked different ritual specialists to repeat the verses slowly. I again recorded the verses by hand through use of the International Phonetic Alphabet and standard linguistic field techniques. Then I made a word-for-word translation from Dusun into English and Malay. I proceeded finally to make a free translation of the word-for-word translation, using English syntax and grammar structure to express the ideas inherent in the Dusun verses. All the verses used in this text have been translated in this fashion.

the baby's chest, and severs it with the bamboo knife. She then covers the navel area with a preparation made from leaves of jungle plants. The baby is wrapped by the midwife in one of its mother's skirts, then placed between kapok-filled pillows at the edge of the mat on which the mother is still kneeling.

The midwife assists the mother in the expulsion of the placenta by gentle massage of the uterus. When the placenta has been fully expelled, the midwife takes it up in a bamboo section, which is about 12 inches long and 3 to 4 inches in diameter, closed at one end and with small holes cut in the sides near the bottom. The midwife then places the cord, placenta, and bamboo knife into the bamboo container. The container is passed to the father, who ties it closed with a large leaf held in place by a piece of split bamboo or rattan, then takes it to the side of the house on the upper side of the hill and hangs it under the house eaves, where it serves as public announcement of birth. The tube remains there until taken down by the child when he is old enough to climb and untie it, or until the rattan used to secure it rots and it falls. The contents of the tube are considered part of the infant's body and to be his property to dispose of as he chooses. The Dusun believe that the infant will be afflicted with a particular type of lifelong misfortune that comes from discarding his cord and placenta rather than placing these things to hang outside the house. The number of containers outside a house are considered by many Dusun as important marks of the parents' status as adults. When a family moves the bamboo containers may be carried with them to the new house and rehung in the outside eaves.

After the cord, placenta, and knife are placed into the bamboo tube, the mother frees herself from the barkcloth strap and lies on her back alongside the infant. If she has postnatal hemorrhage, she is given the hot broth of chicken and rice and has her abdomen bound tightly with the cloth strap she has prepared. A pad of clean cloth may also be used to help staunch the hemorrhaging. Perinal tears are not repaired even if the wound is large. From time to time in the hours after delivery the midwife feels the uterus to see if it is contracting. She also supervises the changing of pads to staunch hemorrhage and the administration of broth given the mother.

The average length of labor witnessed in our studies of birth in the two Dusun communities was about 9 hours for six women undergoing second or subsequent births. Four women bearing their first children were in the first stages of labor for an average of 10 hours, and in the second stage of labor for another 3 hours. One woman bearing her first child was in labor for a total of 20 hours. Since women use no anesthetic in delivery, there is a great deal of pain, which is manifested in the forms of a stylized moaning and sharp, short whimpers as stabs of pain from labor shoot through the uterus. Dusun women are not supposed to be stoical and quiet in labor. The pains of labor and birth are believed to be indicators of the transition to womanhood; and although no woman says she likes or seeks such pain, all mothers interviewed were proud of their ability to bear the pains of childbirth.

The exuviae, or products of birth, are cleaned up by the midwife and given to the father to dispose of in the jungle. Soiled clothing and most articles used in delivery are taken to the river to be washed by the father or the mother's mother.

The mat used for delivery must be retained, for it is believed a woman will bear no more children if it is destroyed. It is considered bad for any other person to dispose of exuviae or clean the mother's personal effects. If an unmarried boy or girl disposes of the birth products because the husband is absent or ill, they must pay the mother a special "cooling" fine of one chicken and 1 yard of cloth or they will supposedly suffer the penalty of sterility at marriage. If other persons touch the mother's effects used in birth before they are washed, this fine is doubled. Such persons are believed to have endangered their own children as well as having been made barren by the act. Mothers cleanse themselves with hot water when they are able to do so after the delivery.

Midwives are given a ritual payment to insure a "cooling" of the fortune of the child and the midwife. It is believed that birth attracts harmful supernaturals and forces. The ritual payment consists of goods, usually a small amount of cloth, salt, a small measure of rice, and one hen. The midwife is allowed to keep the hen and its chicks to insure the mother will increase the numbers of her children as the hen does her chicks. This is one of the few instances where an animal paid as part of ritual fine is not killed and eaten by the ritual specialist.

Difficult and unusual births are explained as a failure of the mother to observe proper behavior during conception or pregnancy or as the consequence of sickness or some peculiar events experienced by mother in pregnancy. Thus, breech births are explained as being caused by a mother sleeping on one side all through pregnancy; the baby turns about so the head is upward. Abnormal presentations are sometimes treated by a ritual used for general and serious illness. Deformed children are said to be due to the carrying of heavy loads, or violation of one of the prenatal taboos. Birthmarks are said to be caused by a mother sewing with black-dyed thread during her pregnancy, or eating red or black nuts or berries before birth of the child. Birthmarks are considered a sign of good luck for growth and strength; people other than parents will exclaim on sight of a birthmark, "There is a good luck for him [her] in life." Premature births are feared because they are viewed as an "unlucky" omen and are believed to be the consequence of the mother breaking some one of the pregnancy and conception taboos, especially those concerned with avoidance of certain animal signs or sounds. Premature babies are given no special treatment to aid them to survive. Caul births are believed to provide an invincibility to illness, accident, and death in war.[4] Caul births are considered so special that as an adult, the "caul person," whether a ritual specialist or not, is asked "to draw out" illness in a person by using their fingers to locate and extract the object causing sickness. Caul membranes are considered by parents as signs of an infant's invincibility. Caul persons are said to be "the best" persons for ritual specialists and war and political leaders. A baby is "left in" the caul membrane until it rots off; openings are made for the eyes, nostrils, mouth, and ears under a belief that impairment of these senses results from leaving them covered.

Stillbirths are explained as the consequence of the mother's blood cooling just before delivery, usually as the result of her violating some taboos of pregnancy.

[4] The inner fetal membrane of higher vertebrates sometimes is not ruptured at birth and so covers the head of the baby until cleared away.

Stillbirths are usually buried immediately by the father, at an unmarked loction some distance into the jungle. An alternative practice is to bury the dead infant under the house, near the steps, under the belief that it is still part of the mother's body and should be near her place of daily life.

Deformed and obviously retarded infants are generally feared and cause great emotional stress for the parents and their families. Deformations and retardation is supposed to result from a serious violation of the taboos of conception and pregnancy. Husbands of women bearing a deformed child say they "feel very ashamed," especially if the infant is a first child, since this is taken to mean a lifetime of "bad luck" for the parents.[5]

Multiple births, especially of triplets, are disliked and feared, for they are also believed to be the result of violation of conception and pregnancy taboos. A general explanation given for twins is that a mother has worked so hard that the fetus divided into two parts, or that a mother has fallen so hard that she has broken the fetus in half. A pregnant woman is supposed to be able to tell of twins by a special pigment mark across her abdomen and the presence of lines of pigment down her inner forearms. The absence of feeling in the breasts and nipples before birth is also taken as an indication of twins. Same-sexed twins are viewed with less distaste than opposite sexed twins. Opposite sexed twins are believed to be a brother and sister who have been living together in an "unclean" way in the uterus.

No form of infanticide, or the killing of a newborn child, is now regularly practiced by the Dusun. In the recent past, some infants born of incestuous relationships were put to death on judgment of a village council. It was said to be a common practice to place the infant in a large bamboo container, then bury the child alive to kill it by suffocation. It was also reported by older informants that occasionally the infant was banished from the community with his parents or taken from his mother and given to a childless couple to raise as their own, once the adopting parents had paid the proper ritual fine to "cool" the offense caused to the community by the act of incest. "Incest children" are those infants born of sexual acts between parent-child, brother-sister, children of a man's several wives, and between persons known to be related within the third degree in the father's and mother's line of descent.

Illegitimate children are jokingly called "children of stone." It is said that because there is no known father, the illegitimate child must be attributed to the "stone people" of long ago.[6] The Sensuron and Baginda midwives reported an average of two illegitimate births each year in each community. Illegitimate children are considered "bad" for the luck of the parents and the families of the parents because no dowry has been paid by the father to the mother's father and there has been no return of the symbolic payment usually made by the bride to the groom's father. These payments and the marriage feast are indicators of the formal alliance of the *teŋran* of the parents and notations of the vital importance of

---

[5] An infant born with a cleft palate (a congenital palative fissure forming one cavity for the nose and mouth) is not considered as "unlucky" since it will speak as an adult with the same voice attributed to the creator beings.

[6] The term is also used because of the feeling that since the child has no dowry "working for him," he is as stone is, since "it never works for its food."

marriage in Dusun life. If a girl does not know, or will not tell, the name of the child's father, the midwife can try to determine his identity by calling out the names of suspects as labor proceeds, finally making the identification from the name she has called out as the baby is fully delivered of the mother. On occasion the mother is made to call out the names of suspected fathers as she delivers. The mother is warned that the infant will "grab hold" of her heart and refuse to be born and kill her unless she cooperates in identifying the father. A married woman cannot have an "illegitimate" child. She may have a child by a man other than her husband, but unless the husband makes a public issue of the matter, it is a moot point. If the issue is raised by her husband, she is fined for adultery. The mother of an illegitimate child may be made to appear before the village council and pay a fine to "cool" her offense to the community. Usually, the fine is one grown pig. She can be brought to the attention of the council by any older married woman, or her mother, who are supposed to feel aggrieved by her offense. The man named as the father is made to pay a similar fine and is asked to marry the girl. If he cannot, or will not, do so, he is made to pay the full dowry the girl's father had expected at her marriage. If the ritual fines are paid and the couple marries, or if the child's father pays the expected dowry, the infant is received in the community as is any other child. If the fines and the dowry are not paid, the mother and child are often treated as outcasts in the community and made objects of open ridicule, scorn, and derision by adults and children. The life of an illegitimate child in a Dusun community is more difficult than that of an adult judged guilty of murder; under traditional law a murderer could "replace" his victim in the community with the equivalent of the victim's life in goods, then bear no further stigma for the act. An illegitimate child cannot escape the consequences of his parent's act. Through his life he bears the mark of their refusal to abide by expected behavior; he will find it difficult to marry, to be considered a responsible adult, and will be the focus of fear and accusations and suspicions of poisoning and magical harm.

If a woman dies in childbirth and the infant lives, her mother or her husband's mother will care for it until it is two to three years old. The father pays for the support of the infant while he maintains his house and cares for any older children. The death of a mother usually is blamed on her "bad luck." Thus, the motherless infant is not mistreated, or given less regard or care because of his mother's death.

A new mother is supposed to rest for a period of two to four days while she eats special foods to "nourish her blood." The first food given to her is a broth made from boiling one of a number of jungle plants which are supposed to stimulate the flow of her milk. This is prepared with rice and salt by the midwife and is often served by the father. If the breast milk flows early and well, the broth is eaten only once. If the milk does not come, the food is served until it does so. A broth made of chicken, rice, and ginger is boiled by the father and served by him as the mother requests it "to build her blood strong." A new mother is not allowed to eat any "hanging" fruits or vegetables, particularly blackberries, jackfruits, cucumber, breadfruits, and must avoid all deer meat. These foods are supposed to cause a new mother to have "pains," "fevers," and jungle ulcers or to become a victim of leprosy. Pork is considered "too oily" for a new mother, as is the flesh of the duck. Generally the postparturient mother cares for her own body needs. If she is very ill from the effects of delivery, she is cared for until well by the midwife or her mother or by her husband.

In the first hours after delivery, a lengthy ritual is performed by a female ritual specialist to protect the mother from harm by "disease givers" and "souls of the dead" drawn to her by the "smell of birth" deriving from her lochia flow. The ritual specialist offers a chicken as "food" for the harmful spirits in an attempt to bribe them away from the mother's body, and employs the odor of a cultivated marsh root to attempt to drive away these spirits. This ritual comprises approximately one hundred verse lines, chanted in about one hour. On completion of the ritual the mother is isolated to sleep until she wakes and requests food.

It was noted at the beginning of the chapter that knowledge of the details of beliefs and behavior involved in conception, pregnancy, and childbirth are vital for understanding the way a people value children, view physical maturation, and prepare for the many social changes which occur when a child is born. The data included in this chapter are intended to provide insights into the ways Dusun adults are involved in the process of enculturation from a time well before the birth of a child to the act of birth itself. These beliefs and practices provide a specific setting within which young adults are prepared to become parents and to be responsible for the utterly dependent infant. It can be easily overlooked that young adults are not equipped with biologically fixed, specific characteristics which lead them to behave properly and with wisdom at the time they become parents. This descriptive account of the prenatal beliefs and acts of Dusun parents provides some ways of understanding how Dusun learn to be parents. It is my belief that these many acts, which seem quite disparate, are related to the process of teaching adults to be parents.

4 / Infancy

THE MAJOR EVENTS in the first year of a Dusun child's life are discussed in this chapter. These events provide impetus and direction to the traditional patterns of enculturation which occur in the time from the second year to adolescence.

A Dusun infant is born into a culture of great complexity. Adult concepts of the universe, the natural world, of life and death, health and disease, fortune and misfortune, and of justice, truth, authority, property, kinship, social organization, subsistence, and material culture are defined in great detail and interwoven in an intricate, delicately balanced, and functionally related set of patterns of and for personal behavior. Dusun adults are especially concerned with the nature and activities of some 40 named supernatural beings known to cause personal ill fortune, sickness, accident, and death. Dusun depend upon an involved and finely detailed system of cultural· explanations of beneficial supernatural beings and forces and formal and personal ritual acts to counter the influence of the harmful supernaturals. The ritual acts are associated with an extensive body of ritual verse.

As an infant matures in Dusun society, his life becomes increasingly more concerned with and caught up in the extensive network of patterns of formal and personal ritual, until as an adult, he will be conscious most of every day of the place and meaning of ritual in his life.[1] The sights and sounds of ritual specialists, both male and female, become a part of his life, as they seek out supernatural agencies of harm and attempt to deal with them through substitutions of food or goods for the victim, withdraw objects from a victim's body, or through verse to frighten or lure away from a victim the harmful beings which afflict him. Also, a child becomes increasingly involved in the extensive preparations for ritual acts as he grows older.

RITUAL IN INFANCY

It can be said that almost the first sounds a Dusun is exposed to at his birth, and nearly the last ones "heard" at his death, are those from the verses softly chanted

---

[1] Personal ritual acts are those which individuals engage in to protect themselves as they encounter a situation (such as a muddy place, a rainbow), an omen (bird calls, sights of certain animals), or take part in an event (an accidental death, a fight which can bring personal harm from one of the malevolent spirit beings). There are some 15 brief ritual sayings and more than 50 ritual curses to be used in such situations.

by a female ritual specialist. As the newborn lies on his back on the mat onto which his mother has delivered him, the words of the ritual of *pèpèdsu nàtàduàn,* which is said to protect his mother from harmful spirits, come down to him from the kneeling female specialist; with her ceremonial headdress swinging gently as she rocks back and forth on her knees, she begins intoning the first of 50 verse lines to aid the mother.

In the first month or so of his life, a Dusun infant undergoes an eight- to ten-day period of ritual isolation with his mother and may be subjected to as many as 12 formal and usually lengthy rituals. Each of these ritual acts is concerned with some aspect of life adults see as vital to the health and growth of the baby.

Isolation in the household for the infant and mother occurs for an eight- or ten-day period after birth. Both periods involve the mother and child being kept from contact with all family members except the husband, the woman's mother, her husband's mother, and a female ritual specialist. Any other adults than these persons must pay a ritual fine for entering the household. The fine traditionally is one chicken, one small porcelain cup, and one measure (half-coconut shell) of swidden rice. The child undergoing ritual isolation at birth cannot be carried outside of the house into the "rays of the sun" under the belief that he will get a fever and die; the heat of the sun is believed to especially attract to it the soul (*rusèd dè tànàk*) of the infant. Proof of this attraction is said to be found in the heat in the belly of an infant when it is taken into the sun in the first eight to ten days after its birth. It

As primary social unit neighbors look on, the author's wife bandages a head cut for a six-year-old boy.

Five female ritual specialists chant verses during a ceremony to insure good luck for a neighborhood while younger girls listen and observe. The specialist costume has been the traditional Sensuron woman's dress in the recent past.

is also felt to be very harmful to the infant to have a "stranger," that is, someone other than the father, mother's mother, father's mother, or a female ritual specialist, walk upon the infant's sleeping mat, or touch its person. This is supposed to lead to a final soul loss and death.

On the second or fourth day after birth, a female ritual specialist comes to the house of the newborn and performs a lengthy ritual (*pègedu sèmubu*) which is intended to placate harmful supernaturals made angry by their inability to get at the mother's milk because of the flow of colostrum from her breasts the first days after delivery.[2] It is believed the baby may be harmed by malevolent beings unable to attack the mother. The ritual act involves a series of approximately twenty lines of verse, repeated while a chicken is offered by the female ritual specialist to lure the harmful spirit beings from the mother and child and verses giving threats of harm by the creator beings to the malevolent spirits if they do not withdraw from the household. At the completion of the ritual, the chicken is killed and cooked as food for the mother.

On the fourth or sixth days after delivery, the child is subjected to a second ritual (*làntàdàk*; *mèmèlàntàdàk*; *pèmègèmpe dè tànàk*). The ritual is intended to "accustom" the baby to his new home and is said by a female specialist to protect the infant from harm as he is carried about within the house. A newborn ideally cannot

---

[2] Colostrum is a secretion from the lactiferous glands of the breasts before the onset of true lactation.

be moved from the mat onto which he was delivered until this ritual has been repeated. The female ritual specialist kneels on the mat before the child and chants this set of verses:

I will take up these dried leaves I have gathered to accustom the child to his world.

Look! Look at the dried leaves, which have dropped from the great jungle trees!

No one has touched their bodies.

And so it is and will be with this child.

No one, including any kinds of spirits, can get hold of or touch this child!

A third ritual act is also performed for the child on the fourth or sixth day after his birth. This form (*mènèduk dè tànàk*; *mànèled*; *mènànènsàlud*) involves a ritual covering of the infant in a garment supposed to have magical powers. It is usually said just after completion of the *làntàdàk* ritual. Some mothers feel it best to separate the two rituals by one day to avoid "confusing the spirits." There are two versions used by Dusun. The more common form is comprised of the following verses:

Come out, children [spirits], come out, children!

Come look at this baby!

As her three-year-old son listens, a mother chants a ritual verse to her dying newborn son.

He is not dead!

You must get used to him.

I will journey along the jungle path with the baby, so you can look at him.

As we pass by, you can look at him, but you will see that I have covered his head with the *sènduk* to protect him.

Let this chicken represent the headcloth now wrapped around him.

You can take the chicken to become accustomed to him.

Now you cannot say you do not know him!

Now, listen!

The jungle dwellers reply!

We have looked upon this baby as you asked.

Hand over the chicken, which is like the headcloth, and we will become used to this baby being on our jungle path, and will not harm him.

We give you the power to make him wise and strong.

As he was born easily, so he will grow easily, with no sickness or accident.

He will grow into adulthood for we have taken off the lid which holds back growth.

He will be cool and steady and grow without sickness.

As the female ritual specialist chants these verses she holds the child and wraps it in her headcloth (*sènduk*) to impart its magical powers to the child.

On the eighth, tenth, twelfth, or fourteenth days after birth the mother and child have the ritual (*pèpèdsu dè tau orintud*) said by the female specialist to protect them from harm by malevolent beings as they leave their protective isolation. Using "sacred water," the female specialist says these verses over the infant as the mother holds it in her arms:

What shall I receive for this sacred water?

That sacred water which is not affected by ill fortune!

There are many streams running down to the river.

And, so the river does not dry up, it floods so high instead that all ill fortune is washed away.

The river also reflects ill fortune from its surface.

The rice can be made safe by sacred water.

Everyone who sows the seed in the nursery of rice, all those who touch and hold the rice, do not bring it ill fortune because the sacred water reflects it away from them.

The sacred water has become famous over the generations of our people; for as many generations as men can remember we have had more good fortune than any strangers.

So, for countless generations to come in an infinite number there will be good fortune, brought by the sacred water.

It will flood away and reflect all ill fortune from us!

This ritual is the infant's introduction to the adult beliefs in events of ill fortune that can be altered or directed by uses of formal ritual involving "sacred water." As he matures, the individual will come to use sacred water as a prime means of dealing personally with bad luck or to insure future good fortune. It will be one of the "lucky" objects he carries with him. It will hang in containers on his house and be used as an integral part of more than half of all Dusun formal ritual. When this ritual is completed, the infant may be carried out of the house as the mother resumes her work.

On the twentieth or twenty-second day after delivery a ritual (méŋarèŋèb dè genauè; pèmèmèràŋeb; pèmèmgàḳut) is performed by the female specialist to shape and direct the maturation of the infant's character and reason. It is usually said with only the mother and child present. Although there may be other members of the family in the household after the ending of ritual isolation, they tend to avoid ritual acts known to help in protecting the new child because they believe their presence would alter the ritual. Again, sacred water is a vital part of the ritual. As the female specialist rubs sacred water onto the chest and the top of the infant's head, she says these verses:

I take this sacred water, which I shall use to loose the tight lid of the pot, to pick up the cover of that vessel!

I say that this one's character and reason are not complete.

But as I bathe him with the sacred waters, it will begin on its way to being complete.

Even if this house about us is left alone, it will be safe because of the sacred waters which protect it.

So the body of this one will be protected by sacred waters even though a soul leaves him for a while.

His body and souls will grow together, and he will be protected then.

He will be tempered as is this iron in my hand! Strong!

The posts of his body will be like iron!

They will support him as he grows strong, with reason and character of iron!

It is believed this vital ritual frees and strengthens the character and reason of the child for growth toward the "time of reason" at seven to eight years. Without the ritual a child can be sickly in body and "mind" and become short tempered, a rascal, a boaster, and a wanderer. There is no conception, however, that the ritual fully provides character or reason for the infant in such a manner that he can subsequently be treated as a responsible and responsive social entity. As has been noted, Dusun adults do not feel infants and young children are possessed of reason. It is believed that reason develops as the body matures and as the child's souls become "experienced" in life. The ritual is repeated on the first birthday of the child and ideally should be said once a year, in the midyear, each year until a child is judged "to be with reason." It is also believed that the ritual should be said at times of critical illness which may affect reason. Most children have this ritual said for them at the time of their birthdays up to the age of four years. It is felt that these special rituals to promote growth and strength of reason are the responsibility of the father and his *teŋran* group. The arrangements and payments to the ritual specialist for her services are made and paid for by the father on behalf of his *teŋran* group. A common Dusun expression is, "A child's reason is the responsibility of his father's *teŋran.*

Ritual specialists are supposed to be paid a fee for their services. The fee paid and the manner of payment varies with the nature and intent of the ritual, the wealth of the family of the affected person, and the circumstances of the ritual. In most rituals used in conception, pregnancy, and birth and for growth and protection the fee involves payment of rice, small amounts of salt, eggs, and a fowl, with the inclusion of a yard or two of cloth, or perhaps some tobacco. Today a few Malay dollars may be used in lieu of some of the more traditional payments. The schedule of payment for ritual has no relation to the effects of divination or treatment, except in a very general way; a large payment does not guarantee immediate cure, but it is felt wise to pay the specialists well to avoid causing them magical harm (or *tàpun*) by neglecting to honor their skills, refusing them hospitality and thereby changing their personal luck.

SOCIAL PLACEMENT

The sixth ritual an infant undergoes in the first month of his life takes place on the thirtieth or thirty-second day from birth. This form (*mègèndàha dè tapini*; *mèmèrug*; *mègèdèn dè tànàk*; *mèŋedu dè pàtàgèn*) involves the infant being carried by his mother or one of his mother's sisters to the household of his mother's father and mother. This is a formal observance of the infant's affiliation to the *teŋran* of his mother and is intended to "show" the child these relatives and to provide opportunity for the relatives to ceremonially join in the act of rearing the child. Like all others in the first month of the infant's life, this ritual must be performed on an even-numbered day, because even numbers added together are believed lucky. Odd numbers added together are felt to be extremely unlucky. If odd numbers are used for any event which affects the child, it is felt that "he will always be sick."

When the child arrives at his mother's father's home, he is welcomed by his mother's mother and father at the steps and carried by his grandfather into the the house. Here a ritual specialist or the mother's mother says the ritual verses while the child is held in the arms of his mother's father, or his mother's father's father, the representative of the mother's *teŋran*. The verses are as follows:

> I swear in the name of the creator force that
> I will loosen the new generation of this *teŋran*
> so it will leap up, growing in health, being
> turned aside by no enemies!

> Nothing will detain this generation, make it thin
> or a sickly color, give it a bad feeling, or
> make its body rotten.

> And bad luck will be cleared away now! I
> look closely at this new generation of the *teŋran*
> and I make it cry lustily! There! See
> now nothing will hold it back!

After the ritual is completed, a period of several hours of feasting occurs, and then the female ritual specialist or mother's mother says one of three rituals to "loosen" or "untie" the growth of the infant. These forms (*mèŋedu dè pàtàgèn; sumèndele; pèmumeueàd dè tànàk*) are used at the option of the grandparents. An important aspect is the tying onto the infant of objects supposed to have magical powers. A female infant has a small silver bell attached to a thin silver-wire ring slipped onto her right ankle, while a small seashell button, attached to a piece of string, is tied about her left wrist. A male infant has the same objects placed on his left ankle and right wrist. These objects are believed to bring increased growth to the child. They are supposed to be worn until children outgrow them at two-and-one-half to three years, or they are lost in play. The objects are not replaced if lost. Before the ritual is said, strings are temporarily tied on the other wrist and ankle of the infant and then cut off by the specialist as she chants the ritual verses:

> I swear in the name of the creator force that I untie the growth, loosen the growth of this child.

> He is not yet loosened to grow and not yet strong of soul, but I will untie him from the bonds that hold him.

> There will be no impurities of talk that can hold back his growth! No impurities of talk!

> There will be those that will be jealous of the way this child will grow, and they will speak badly of him.

> But they must beware! For I have sworn to put the growth of the creators into him.

> I have unloosened his soul and body so they had best beware!

> They had better not try to steal his soul, or poison him with their impurities of talk!

Make this child grow as the stalk of rice, tall and strong and well.

Loosen the shoot in him!

Let him grow fast and well!

Let him grow faster than all other children and be healthier and stronger!

On occasion the ritual specialist will hang a small empty knife scabbard about a female infant's neck, or a knife blade about a male infant's neck to induce conception of another child for the mother.

This ritual observance is believed to "introduce" the baby to the property paid at marriage by the groom to the father of the bride, which stays in the mother's house "to keep her parents company and to work [for example, to earn interest and be used as collateral in loans] in her place." If a child enters his mother's father's house before this ritual is performed, it is felt he will sicken and die. If a woman's parents are dead, and she has no brothers or sisters to hold the ritual, then the property given at marriage is taken from her house to that of a close friend and the ceremony is held there.

Sometimes the infant's mother's father may come to the household during the time the ritual specialist is saying the *làntàdàk* ritual on the fourth or sixth day after birth and he repeats the verses (quoted previously) when the specialist has completed her recitation. The mother's father holds the child in his arms as he softly chants the verses. When the mother's father says these verses, the ritual is termed *pèmègèmpe dè tànàk*. Dusun say their "feeling" concerning the new child being made aware of and part of his mother's *teŋran* is so strong that if the mother's father waits until the usual time of the *mègèndàha* ritual, there is a possibility the child will treat his mother's *teŋran* as "strangers" and become sick through fear of contact with them. Thus the mother's father usually breaks into the ritual isolation to try to insure that the infant is familiar with his mother's *teŋran* as well as his father's *teŋran*. Although the father's father does not visit with the child in the first two weeks of its life, it is presumed that since the child is born in his father's house, he is already familiar with his father's *teŋran*.

On an even-numbered day sometime in the two weeks after the observance of the *mègèndàha* ritual with the mother's *teŋran,* an abbreviated form of the same ritual may be repeated at the household of the father's parents. Here, the father's *teŋran* gather to "meet" the infant. The ritual verses and acts of placing objects during *mèŋedu dè pàtàgèn* are not usually repeated, since promotion of the infant's growth is believed reserved for the mother's *teŋran*. During the feasting which occurs at this ritual observance, it is common for the father's relatives to repeat a brief "good luck" comment to the infant as they hold and fondle him, and hand over presents to the mother to "welcome" the baby to the *teŋran*. This observance at the father's father's home is often treated as a first-month birthday party or "he comes to one month of life." The ritual acts formally complete the process of alliance of the two *teŋran* each parent represents. At the birth of the first child, the *teŋran* become merged and assured of continuity. The acts of the first-month birthday celebration are usually repeated on the infant's first-year birthday and fifth-year birthday by his nuclear family. The infant's father's *teŋran* are especially invited to these observances. If the family is very poor, only the midwife or ritual specialist in attendance at the child's birth and the father's father and mother are present at the celebrations. If the family is wealthy, all of the father's *teŋran* are also invited to these celebrations. If the family is very wealthy in rice, both the father's and mother's total *teŋran* are asked to celebrate the birthdays. A vital part of these observances is the ritual offering of food and a small gift by the child's mother to the midwife or ritual specialist. The mother silently passes the gift and food to the midwife as an indicator of the other woman's symbolic "ownership" of her baby. Dusun say, "The midwife sees the infant first, so she forever owns him as her own." The gift and food giving is viewed as symbolic of the good health to come for the child, and the midwife's presence at the occasion of the first-month, first-year, and fifth-year birthdays is felt to insure continued good health and fortune for the child.

At the time of the first-month birthday observance, the hair of an infant is trimmed by its father in a simple ritual act (*mèdsubàk dè mènineko*). While the midwife, or female ritual specialist, holds the baby, the father silently and carefully cuts off all hair on the head except a small square covering the spot over the anterior fontanel, which is believed to be the location of soul exit and disease entry.[3] The cut hair is gathered and given to the mother. She sometimes places it in the bamboo container which holds the umbilical cord, for it is believed that the hair is part of the products of conception and birth, since it grew while the child was in the womb. Sometimes the hair is placed in a separate container and discarded by burying or burning because "it came from inside the mother." Ideally, the infant is not supposed to sleep in another household until this act has taken place. The cutting of a child's hair subsequent to this ritual involves no special ceremony or acts. The small patch of hair is left on the heads of many boys until they are about five years old. A particular style of haircutting for little girls is also used until they are about five years old. The meaning and function of this haircut is the same as the patch of boy's hair, but the form is different; little girls are allowed to have their hair grow in thickly back of a transverse line on the skull across the anterior fontanel spot. In front of this line the head is shaved or the hair cut very close to the scalp. Thus little boys can have shaven or close-cropped heads except for the small patch of hair, while little girls can have a full head of hair except for the shaved or close cropped area in front of a line across the center forehead.

If a couple has been childless for a number of years and then they have a child, they are obliged to hold a feast for both personal *teŋran* and members of their mutual aid groups, neighborhood, special friends, and the politically and ritually important persons in their village descent group. This requirement often makes a poor family assume large debts in order to secure enough rice for food and drink. The celebration, termed "to give thanks for having a child," is viewed as the necessary obligation of the parents for having benefited from the skills of a female ritual specialist in divining the nature of their sterility and from the general good

---

[3] Fontanel means a space, or "soft spot," of unossified bone between sutures of the skull in a fetus and infants. The anterior fontanel is located at a spot in the top center of the forehead.

fortune of their friends and neighbors, which canceled out, or suspended, the parents' bad fortunes. During this celebration, which may last two to five days, the infant is "introduced" to nearly everyone at the affair in the belief that its good luck will bring each participant more personal fortune.

At the times of the celebrations by the mother's *teŋran* and the father's *teŋran*, it is considered good manners for each adult guest to give a small present to the infant as a symbol of their hopes for its continued good fortune. Presents usually consist of cloth or a measure of rice.

INFANT CARE

The Dusun use the term *mègunàk* to denote the act of caring for a child. The term can be translated as including the meanings of (1) "to raise," (2) "to rear," (3) "to physically care for," and (4) "to teach the right ways." This term is used also to describe a woman nearly ready to deliver. Dusun believe that the act of *mègunàk* begins with conception and ends with a child's marriage. There are three aspects of this concept which are believed especially vital to the growth, health, and good fortune of an infant: (1) *mènumàd* ("to feed a child"), (2) *mèmèdsu* ("to bathe a child"), and (3) *mèmurès* ("to instruct with words"). Feeding and cleaning are considered the prime tasks of parents until a child matures enough at seven or eight years to be given specific instructions. The act of caring for or "minding" a child is termed *mintàmèŋèn*. Specific concern with protecting a child from dangerous events and locations is expressed in the term *lànsànàn*. These two terms are most commonly used by Dusun adults in talking about care of a child of two years or older and are also part of the definition of the concept of *mègunàk*. When Dusun adults use the general term *mègunàk*, they usually mean all five aspects of the care of children, that is, to feed, bathe, instruct, mind, and protect from dangers.

A mother spends most of her time in the first month and much of her time in the first six months after birth caring for an infant. She judges the baby's need for feeding or bathing from the heat of the area of the anterior fontanel; mothers touch their thumb or forefinger tips to this area to see if the skin is "cool" or "hot." A "cool" fontanel is considered a sign of a healthy baby. A "hot" fontanel is believed an indication of illness. In the first month of a child's life, the physical care he receives is directly related to the heat of the anterior fontanel. If the child is "cool," he probably will not be fed until he fusses and likely will not be bathed until he becomes dirty. Between the end of the eight- to ten-day ritual isolation period and before the infant is taken to visit its mother's *teŋran* for the ritual of *mègèdàha*, a beeswax preparation is applied to the anterior fontanel area in the belief that "sickness cannot escape the sticky wax." This preparation is regularly placed over the anterior fontanel by many mothers to ward off sickness and bad fortune. The baby is believed protected also by a necklace made of a cultivated marsh herb with a pungent rootstock odor ("sweet flag" or *Acorus calamus*). The necklace is felt to have a smell greatly offensive to harmful spirit beings. Mothers try to insure that the infant wears the marsh-root necklace whenever it is carried from the house. Most children regularly wear a necklace or have bits of the root tied to their sleeping

A mother nurses her son as she touches the top of his head to try to determine his body heat.

cover until they are about five years of age. Some mothers also attach a small container of "sacred water" to the baby's clothes to protect it from sickness. Generally Dusun feel that a healthy mother will have a healthy baby and mothers pay careful attention to their own activities as they care for the new child. While she is avoiding carrying the new child out without its magical charms and seeks to keep him from the hot rays of the sun and away from known habitats of harmful spirits (such as mud and muddy places), a mother also gives careful consideration to the omens of fortune affecting her and to signs of her own physical well-being. Mothers of infants readily use the services of a female ritual specialist to divine the nature of events believed likely to affect their health and fortune. The general conception of infancy is that a baby is "not aware of the dangers about him, so mothers have to look out for him."

Dusun infants are nursed as the mother thinks the baby demands feeding. Nursing usually occurs until one breast is dry. Breasts are the primary symbols of maternity to Dusun. A big-breasted woman with large areola and prominant nipples is considered to be fertile and a desirable marriage partner. To stimulate the flow of milk immediately after birth a mother often drinks a number of cups of rice, mixed with hot chicken broth. This is felt to turn the colostrum into milk and to insure adequate lactation. It is believed unwise for a mother to eat anything except the meat of chicken, water buffalo, particular jungle vegetables, and rice served as a hot broth. This food is said to "build the body of the mother and insure much milk." If a mother waiting to nurse a child breaks these food taboos by eating pork, fruits, and domestic vegetables, she is said to be liable to affliction from the supernaturally caused disease of *àuenk̇àt* and eventual death. While waiting for her milk to flow and in the first month of nursing, a mother usually cooks in separate pots and eats apart from the family. Usually a mother eats her food on the spot where she has given birth. During this period the father cooks for himself and the other children and does the washing of his wife's clothes and most other domestic chores. The couple avoid sexual intercourse during this time because they fear *àuenk̇àt*. Ideally such abstention lasts for 40 nights after birth. In reality it may last only two weeks.

If milk does not come to a mother's breasts, she will seek the help of a female ritual specialist to cure her and will begin to prepare a special food as a milk substitute for the infant. A special jungle plant is drained of its stalk juices and this is cooked with rice broth and mixed with sugarcane juices in a potion fed to the infant as a milk substitute. Motherless infants, or infants of dry-breasted women, are given this preparation until they thrive or die. It is very unusual for an infant to be wet nursed by another woman.[4] Milk is considered so much a part of the mother's body, and natural being, that Dusun find it difficult to comprehend the concept of a wet nurse. It is said by Dusun, "It is bad to have a baby suck at another breast because the woman is afraid the infant is a *naro susu* in the guise of a baby." The *naro susu* (or *sedutsedut*) is pictured as a very small evil spirit with the appearance of a man, except for a mouth with teeth specially adapted to biting and sucking the breasts of nursing mothers. These beings are said to feed by emptying one breast while blocking the nipple of the other breast with a hand to keep the infant from eating. The most common explanation for infant death is a *naro susu* emptying a mother's breasts.

A newborn infant is induced to nurse by forcing the nipple into his mouth while the mother sharply says, "Suckle! Suckle!" A newborn who refuses to nurse is said to be not yet fully born, or "grown." Infants are supposed to know how to nurse because it is believed they suck their thumb in the womb to eat hot blood to cause fetal growth. Mothers are suprised and concerned when a newborn refuses to nurse, for it is felt that this is a sign that some evil spirit being has taken possession of the child; it is reasoned that since the fetus has grown by sucking, the absence of a sucking reflex is a sign of possession of the child by a spirit or force which does not know how to suck since it has "never been born" or because it is too busy eating away the infant's souls to take time to seek milk as food. If evil spirit possession is suspected, a divination ritual is often undertaken by a female specialist. She

---

[4] An infant whose mother dies at birth is usually cared for by the father's mother as her own child. If a father's mother is dead, or unable to care for the child because of illness or age, the mother's mother will care for the infant. In any case, the father has a first claim to the right to seek out a woman to care for the infant.

may also perform one of several lengthy rituals to "undo" or "restore" the child's ability to nurse.

Infants are supposed to be nursed properly when their mother holds them across her body cuddled in her arms, face to the breast. It is believed that "the bones of the baby are so soft he will grow all twisted around if he is held any other way." Observations of nursing show this ideal pattern is generally used in the first three months of nursing. After that time the infant is nursed as he is held in the carrying sling (see later description) or as he is supported by one arm as he rests in the mother's lap. Mothers often use a breast to pacify a crying child.

If a mother thinks her milk to be "good," as judged from the health of the infant, she may continue to nurse him for 6 months before she begins supplementary feeding with solid foods. If a mother feels her milk bad because the infant is sickly, she will begin feedings at about 3 months of a thick paste of water and rice flour pushed into the infant's mouth on a forefinger. At about 8 months most infants are given bits of soft rice that have been prechewed slightly by the mother. By 9 months bits of rice are pushed into the child's mouth. Before one year of age bits of meat are added to the rice and given to the child. Few vegetables are fed to babies until they are about 15 to 18 months old because it is believed "vegetables give a stomachache to a baby." Cooked cucumbers and long beans sometimes are broken into bits and fed to a child of 12 to 15 months. Supplementary feedings are from the mother's own meal and are given to the child on the mother's fingers.

Most Dusun children are weaned by two years. Some children are weaned early because their mothers are aware they are again pregnant. A few children are weaned because the mother's breasts become dry. Usually the weaning process begins with appearance of the child's first teeth at from five to eight months because of a belief that teeth biting a nipple confuse the mother in distinguishing between the *naro susu* biting of the breasts as they feed and the normal action of an infant nursing. Mothers are afraid that a child with teeth will bite a nipple and suck blood rather than milk. If a woman has become pregnant again, the weaning process is viewed as critical to prevent the infant from sucking hot blood and the "steam" forming the fetus. It is believed that the fact nursing children grow thin and sickly when their mothers are pregnant again is evidence of the harm which comes from nursing on "hot blood."

The usual techniques of weaning involve changing the child's sleeping place at home, sending it to spend the night with the father's mother, covering the breasts to make them inaccessible to the child, or use of bitter-tasting food substances on the nipples. Also, the attempts of the child to nurse may be met with loud and scornful comments by the mother. Most often weaning begins by putting the child to sleep with its father while the mother sleeps on another part of the house floor. The child is only sent to sleep with the father's mother if other techniques of weaning seem not to be successful. During the day a mother weaning a child will wear a blouse pulled across her breasts rather than leave her chest exposed as is her normal style of dress. If the child constantly fusses for a breast during the second or third day of weaning, some mothers (approximately two of ten) apply a bitter juice from a jungle vegetable to their nipples and allow the baby to nurse. These mothers may also give the child a stalk of the same bitter vegetable to suck on to discourage attempts to nurse. When a child being weaned grasps at the breasts and attempts to nurse, mothers use a number of stylized expressions to scold them. Commonly used are: "Dirty," "you will suck such bowel worms!" and "you will suck blood!" Many mothers seek to frighten children being weaned with such phrases as: "I shall throw you away!" or "I am afraid to have you take milk for you are already grown; look at all your teeth!" The last phrase implies to the child that he may be possessed by a *naro susu*. Children react to weaning by long crying spells and temper fits and generally show signs of what mothers interpret to be concern and worry. It is not unusual for a mother to scold or shame a child while pushing it from the breast and then to offer gifts of special "sweet food" if the child will stop crying. If none of these techniques of weaning is successful by the end of the fifth to seventh day, the baby is given to the father's mother or mother's mother to feed for a week. The child is also given the "hard" foods described above; "hard food" is comprised of every food except breast milk and the broth fed pregnant and newly delivered mothers and very ill persons. Dusun mothers view the time of weaning as the proper time for the child to begin eating "hard food" by noting, "He must be fed hard food."

Infants are usually exclusively cared for in the first 12 months of their life by their mother. She cleans the baby, disposes of its wastes, clothes and fondles it, and provides conditions for sleep. A mother plays with her baby, provides for its emotional care, protects it from real and supernatural dangers, and helps it with rituals. And a mother carries an infant wherever she goes in her work or leisure time activities.

Dusun believe that "sleep produces growth" in infants. The phrase "sleep is good" is the way mothers express the specific relationship between "growth" and "sleep." In the first 3 months after birth, mothers verbally encourage babies to sleep. When an infant wakes, he is told to rest. When a baby cries, he is instructed to sleep to save his strength to grow on. From birth to 8 months it is believed a baby should sleep from sunset to sunrise without waking and take naps of at least two hours each from three to five times during the day. After 8 months to about 15 months, parents expect the baby to wake at about 3:00 A.M. and sleep only a few hours during the day. A baby or older child that wakes during the night often is scolded by parents with expressions such as, "I do not disturb your sleep—it is still dark and I am still asleep!" Children sleep between their parents from birth until five to seven years or until a new child is born. Then they sleep with other children apart from the parents. Parents say an infant must sleep between them to be properly protected at night. "In the middle between father and mother," they say when asked concerning the "proper" place for a child to sleep.

A mother will try to frighten a baby to put it to sleep. If the child wakes from hearing a sharp sudden noise, such as dogs barking or fowl being stirred up, a mother will comment, "Be quiet! There comes a wildcat to get you!" Parents say, "If a baby becomes very frightened he will keep quiet and sleep." If a baby or young child is restless, his mother or father may say to him, "Go away wildcat!" in a low chant intended to frighten the child into sleep.[5] Mothers regularly sing "lulla-

---

[5] When Dusun adults become very frightened, they tend to become extremely lethargic and stuporous and give the appearance of being intensely weary.

bies" to quiet, soothe, and frighten infants and younger children. Some typical lullabies are:

> Sleep, sleep you baby,
> There is a wildcat on the ground.
> It comes with a bamboo spear,
> A bamboo spear,
> To hit you on the head.
>
> Sleep, sleep you baby.
> There is a wildcat.
> It has a spear and a shield.
> It comes to get you!
>
> Sleep, sleep you baby.
> The wildcat is coming here.
> It carries eggs.
> The eggs of the great hornbill.
> The bird has laid eight eggs for you!

Infants are supposed to be bathed twice a day in tepid water. Most babies are bathed once a day if they are well. If they are mildly sick, the daily bath is given on alternate days. If an infant is very ill, he is not bathed at all. Babies are supposed to be bathed in "hot and cold water" to keep them at a proper temperature while wet. Water is heated over the fire pit and then poured into a vessel with water which is at air temperature. A soap made of coconut-flesh oil is used to wash the infant. The bath begins with the top of the head and proceeds with those body parts said by Dusun to be directly related to infant growth and health: eyes, nose, mouth, ears, chest, underarms, buttocks, back, thighs, ankles, arms, hands, genitals, and feet. In order, these are the parts of the body ideally said to be the "dirtiest" and most in need of bathing. If a baby fusses during the bathing, mothers say, *"è! è! è! è!,"* an exclamatory sound in this case meaning "Quiet!" They may softly repeat the expression "Do not cry!" as they work, or the stylized saying of "You are crying! Yet the dirt is being taken away!" If a mother gets irritated at the baby's crying over being bathed, she may give it a sharp slap on the buttocks, the wrist, or a hand, while commenting to the effect that, "a clean baby grows quickly and is handsome," and "all the people dislike holding a dirty child." Dusun do not like to handle a dirty child since it is believed evil supernaturals are attracted by the smell of the "dirt." It is said by Dusun that "the disease givers can smell the dirt." A few parents allow their children to be dirty under the belief that disease givers, like humans, do not want to eat dirty food. There are several folk tales with themes of people being saved from death by disease givers by rolling themselves in the ashes of a fire or in fecal matter.

Mothers bathe young babies by holding them up with one hand as they kneel on the house floor facing the child. Water and "soap" are dipped out of separate containers and splashed onto the body part being washed. The baby is rinsed off by being splashed with water. Older children are made to stand in a shallow container of tepid water while their mother bathes them. Young babies, to the age of six to eight months, and older children who are suspected of chronic illness, are

A grandmother sings a growth song to her infant grandson.

often bathed in water which has had a jungle-leaf preparation mixed in to cause a "cure" by the aroma it imparts to the water. The juice is believed to smell offensive to disease givers and other harmful spirit beings.

On completion of a bath the infant is dried with the mother's hands, then wrapped in the cloth it has been covered with before the bath. This cloth is rinsed periodically as the mother washes her own clothes at the river.

After a baby has been bathed and wrapped, mothers usually sing several "growth and health songs" to the child. Sitting on the house floor, the mother clasps the baby under the arms, holds it facing her, and repeatedly raises it into the air, then lowers it as she softly sings:

> Bounce, bounce, baby.
> Bounce, bounce the baby.
> I bounce you well, to keep you happy.
> I bounce you quietly, like that hawk
>   who soars high above; like
>   that hawk that swoops low
>   with the frog grasped in his talons.

That big frog!
As the hawk protects you, danger and sickness
    will not harm you,
    and you will be a wise, kind man [woman] full of reason.

Other widely used growth and health songs are:

Bounce, bounce, baby.
There is the eagle, soaring over his reflection.
He carries a big frog, to keep it safe from sickness.
He helps it grow and live all of its life.
He carries a weeding knife to cut down
    the sickness and he uses it.
He cuts down the hot sickness;
    that feverish sickness that affects the child.
He will not allow you to be sick like the others!

Bounce, bounce, baby.
The hawk carries the frog in his claws
To keep him safe from sickness,
To keep him well so he can mature to adulthood.

It is generally believed that unless one growth and health song is sung after each bath, an infant will not grow properly and will become ill. A "good" mother is supposed to use these songs every day, whether or not an infant is bathed.

Mothers allow the child to defecate and urinate freely, giving little attention to the soiling of their own clothing. Usually a mother will wipe the baby's buttocks clean with her hand and then clean the hand on her skirt. Since the Dusun infant wears no diaper, most fecal material goes onto or through the bamboo house floor or the ground under the house. Some Dusun mothers turn the older infant (three to six months) across their knees and allow the family dogs to lick fecal remains from the baby. Dogs usually consume the excreta of children dropped in or near the house, and pigs compete with the dogs. Although a mother may not regularly care for her child's excreta in this manner, at least half of Dusun children have the experience of dogs cleaning them after defecation; when they are between two and four years old and trying to learn to deal with bowel and bladder functions in adult ways, children often are unable to maintain their balance and push away the half-starved dogs fighting about them for excrement.

At the time when the baby begins to sit up alone, between eight and ten months of age, a mother begins to train the child by taking him to the house porch to defecate and urinate. A mother specifically watches the child's expression between eight and ten months to determine whether it may be preparing to relieve itself. If she thinks the infant is about to defecate, she will call out, "è! è! è!" warning a child in this instance not to soil the house, and pick it up and carry it to the edge of the house porch where she repeats several times the phrase, "Have bowel and bladder movements on the porch." This expression is used by parents to older children if they soil the house with feces or urine. If a child looks as if he is squatting to eliminate, this phrase is often shouted at him by a parent or older brother or sister. A common expression to a child soiling the house is a shouted, "Stupid child; you should say you have to defecate-urinate!" Parents allowing infants older than eight to ten months to soil the house with excreta are termed "lazy" and are said to be without reason. Parents say they are "strict" on toilet training because of the possibilities of excreta dirt getting into their food. Dusun consider human adult fecal matter especially potent in causing all kinds of illness. The fecal matter of infants is considered harmless. An adult who smells the feces of other adults can be made sick (for example, made to vomit) by the odor of feces which is *autéŋ* (feces one to three days old) or *ànsud* (feces four to six days old). When an adult is ill and has argued with someone, he usually suspects sickness from contamination with feces and will note, "I have been sick since I smelled that one's feces." Children are regularly warned by parents not to "befoul with feces." Older children use the concept of fouling with feces in their quarrels. A child of three or four learns to "defeat his enemy" by sneaking to the other child's house and defecating on the house floor or under the house. Older children smear their feces on the house posts, as adults do when they try to bring illness through such an act. Young children occasionally defecate during an argument and then throw or try to rub their feces onto another child to make him sick. One of the few times a parent will enter into a child's quarrel is the occasion when their child has had feces smeared upon him. Then a loud and bitter argument may ensue between mothers or fathers of the children. If a child dies after being smeared with feces, the other child's parents may be liable to paying a ritual cooling fine and a substantial fine in property.

If a Dusun baby is not being carried by his mother, father, or another relative, or a child nurse, then he usually lays on his back on the bamboo house floor between two kapok-filled pillows to keep him from rolling, and a kapok pillow to support his head. A kapok filled cover often is tucked about him, sometimes kept in place by the kapok pillows. Usually the parent's woven bamboo sleeping mat is placed under the child. If a baby is picked up by an adult, he is placed in a carrying sling made of a woman's sarong and carried on the adult's back, or astride a hip. The carrying sling is the device used to transport and care for all children to about the age of two years. Children under five years are regularly transported on long journeys in a sling. An infant is placed in the carrying sling in such a fashion as to leave his hands, legs, and head free. Usually a young infant is carried at his mother's or father's front, in an effort to support his head. If a younger child carries an infant, he often slings the baby on his back; it is not unusual to see a three or four year old running hard in play with his infant brother or sister on his back; head and limbs bobbing violently as the game proceeds. Infants and children learn to allow the sling to support them fully. They relax their limbs by letting them hang limply, with feet draped down, toes relaxed and out, and hands held so loosely that the slightest jar causes them to move. It is typical that when Dusun children are held without the support of the sling they do not clutch at the person holding them. They must be held, or they will fall limply away. When an adult plays with, rocks, dandles, distracts, guards, or cares for an infant or younger child, it is usually while the baby is held in a sling. Babies ordinarily become quiet when placed in a sling and often fuss to be carried. It can be said that in the first two to two and a half years of life the Dusun baby spends much of his time being carried in the sling, and in any instance of illness a child under seven or eight years may be cared for and transported by parents while in a sling.

Dusun practice shaping or molding the occipital (back) area of an infant's head. It is believed that this practice, "causes a handsome face," "makes a hat fit properly," and provides "a place for the woman's hair knot to fit." The shaping is conducted by removing the infant's head from the kapok pillow and blocking him tightly to prevent his rolling onto a side. Older children try to sleep on the backs of their heads to insure a flattened occipital area. One adolescent girl stated the relationship between occipital flattening and beauty in her question, "How could you say a man is handsome if he has a round head?"

A child's first clothes consist of the sling he is carried about in, his sleeping cover and a belt made of special tree bark or from a woman's ceremonial head cover. The belt is placed about the baby's body to cover his navel, then tied in a knot in the middle of his back. It is worn as protection against diseases carried on the "bad wind" which get into the belly, and cause pain, fever, and death. Such a wind is believed followed by a harmful supernatural, called *tàmboreè dè taràt,* feared because it enters the bellies of infants to destroy their souls. Since the "bad wind" is possible at all times of the year and is felt to be also responsible for *àuenkàt* as well as several types of usually fatal adult diseases, Dusun pay careful attention to seeing that the infant's belt is put in place immediately after the cord is cut at birth and kept there except during baths. The belt often is tied very tightly about the abdomen under the belief that the tighter the binding, the more effective the protection and elimination of all feeling of pain. A tight bandage is felt most effective for any afflicted body part and any type of pain. Many infants and young children are bound so tightly with a belt that a deep red line 1 to 2 inches wide is left about their body when it is removed. The belt may have bits of marsh root tied to it to protect the infant from harmful supernatural beings. As a baby grows older, he wears only his belt and protective necklaces and amulets until reaching about two to three years of age. A young child may sometimes wear a cast-off hat of his father or mother as he plays near the house. During the years before five, a time designated by the age status terms *iŋà nè tàpe* ("without a skirt") and *iŋà nè sàntud* ("without a loin cloth") for girls and boys, children are not considered immodest when naked except for the belt. As they enter the years from four to five and begin to occupy the age status of *tànàk* ("child"), boys and girls are expected to have "shame" at public display and enough reason to be able to learn by "being able to reflect on one's acts and to be ashamed." Then boys and girls are supposed to regularly wear clothing covering their genitals or face severe public ridicule from neighbors commenting on the child's "boasting" about their sexual powers. The status term *kàtànàkun* ("to be of childhood") is approvingly applied to a child between four and six who regularly covers his genitals. The approbation of *iŋà genauè* ("without reason") is given to children of this age, especially between seven and ten years, who fail to cover their genitals. By eight years of age both sexes are expected to regularly cover their genitals.

INFANT DEVELOPMENT AND MATURATION

Dusun parents recognize and look for particular signs of infant growth and behavior maturation. These signs are believed keys to predicting the future health and personal fortune of the child. In the first year of life there are felt to be 12 signs of growth and behavior maturation. These are:

1. *mèŋènsàlàŋsàlàŋ* "To look up, stare, and be attracted to sound" (ideal age 3 months)
2. *gèmegiŋ* "Learning to roll over" (ideal age 5 to 6 months)
3. *tumiŋèb* "To crawl on the belly crabwise" (ideal age 6 to 7 months)
4. *sumènsàlàŋ* "Creeping with jumping" (ideal age 7 to 8 months)
5. *mètud* "Creeping on hands and knees" (ideal age 1 week after sign 4 occurs)
6. *mèmèŋkàmèŋ* "Creeping" (ideal age 1 week after sign 5 occurs)
7. *merekau* "To sit assisted" (ideal age 1 week after sign 6 occurs)*
8. *kèmàbi* "Holding to stand" (ideal age 1 week after sign 7 occurs—for example, at 8 months)
9. *mèndeleg* "Holding and walking" (ideal age 3 weeks after sign 8 occurs)
10. *mèndelg* "Standing alone, but unsteady" (ideal age 3 weeks after sign 9 occurs)
11. *lèmàŋ* "To step out with hesitation" (ideal age 2 weeks after sign 10 occurs—for example, 10 months)
12. *mèmànau* "To walk alone" (ideal age 12 to 13 months)

Dusun parents recognize that children will not meet all of these standards at all the times expected. If a baby lags slightly behind these expectations, his mother will often provide more frequent nursings, begin to give more solid foods and insist on more sleep for him. If the disparity between these expectations and maturation is a marked one, mothers also will try to provide more food and insist on more sleep and will regularly repeat a ritual promoting more rapid growth as well. This ritual form (*pèmumeueàd dè tànàk*) is repeated once a day by some mothers, and once a week by other mothers, depending on their views of the seriousness of the lag in maturation:

I swear before the creator: Do not choose this one to take!

Untie the spirit of the child and his other souls so he may grow rapidly!

The spirit of this child will be unloosed to allow him to grow well, to grow!

He will not grow pale from sickness or bad fortune as he grows.

He will not have loose bowels, and all parts of his body will be well.

The things that make children sick will not happen to this child.

---

* Dusun parents say the term *merekau* has three aspects: (1) *merekau puenlàtàn*—"to sit with legs extended forward," (2) *gèmèmpepe*—"to sit with legs together, but slanted to one side of the body," and (3) *mèŋnerekau tàkud*—"to sit in a frog squat."

I untie all the growing parts of the body of this child!

I have untied all the bindings that hold back his growth.

He will be well and his body will be free from pain.

He will grow well under the care of his mother.

He will grow and grow, the child will grow and grow.

He will come to no harm, this child of mine.

He will grow and be well!

Few parents choose to ignore failures to mature as expected. If a baby markedly fails to meet the expected standards of maturation, the parents will seek the help of a female ritual specialist to divine the nature of the situation causing slow maturation and to restore the baby's health. Generally the ritual specialist will use one of the many forms of "rituals for sickness" regularly employed in cases of adult illness. Occasionally the parents may ask the ritual specialist to repeat the verses and acts of *mèŋedu dè pàtàgèn* (see previous section, "Social Placement") and then wait several months before saying the much longer ritual forms.

Dusun parents pay little attention to eruption of teeth as a sign of maturation in the first year of life unless the question of weaning becomes a matter of concern. The loss of the first teeth is ritually dealt with by parents.

Description and study of the development and behavior maturation of 14 Dusun infants at various stages in their first year of life shows that Dusun children appear to grow according to the general human schedule of biological development as it has been reported by observers of growth and development.[6]

This was to be expected generally, of course, for within the broad range of individual and local population variations, man comprises a single species. The reason for making a study of Dusun infant maturation in the first year was to determine if there were any significant differences for Dusun children, and if there were, to seek any ways to possibly relate cultural practices in Dusun society (such as care, feeding) to variations in maturation. More intensive studies of maturation, using sophisticated biochemical and metric techniques in a larger sample of Dusun infants may well provide data of growth differences we missed in our preliminary and limited study.

---

[6] For a comparison of Dusun levels of maturation with those expected of American children see, H. K. Silver, C. H. Kempe, and H. B. Bruyn, 1961, *Handbook of Pediatrics*, Los Altos, California, Lange, p. 48. See also, E. H. Watson and G. H. Lowry, 1954, *Growth and Development of Children*, Chicago, Year Book Publishers, pp. 99–104; A. Gesell, and C. S. Amatruda, 1947, *Developmental Diagnosis; Normal and Abnormal Child Development*, New York, Hoeber (2d edition); A. Gesell, 1940, *The First Five Years of Life: A Guide to the Study of the Pre-School Child*, New York, Harper; A. Gesell and F. E. Ilg, 1946, *The Child from Five to Ten*, New York, Harper; and B. Spock, 1946, *The Pocket Book of Baby and Child Care*, New York, Pocket Books.

5 / Childhood years

THE CONVENTIONAL CARE, daily activities, and status of Dusun children from their second year to puberty are described in this chapter.

CHILD CARE

At the end of the first year of a child's life, Dusun parents change their focus of concern within the context of *mègunàk* ("child rearing") from "feeding" (*mènu-màd*), "bathing" (*mèmèdsu*), and "instruction" (*mèmurès*), by lullabies, growth songs, and rituals to concerns with "minding" (*mintàmèŋèn*) and "protecting" (*lànsànàn*) the child.[1] As noted earlier, adults do not feel children are really capable of significant learning before their seventh or eighth year. Adults believe their major task in care for children between two and seven years of age is to make it possible for a child to mature and stay safe from harm. Parents feel that a child can be formally instructed concerning "proper" behavior between 7 and 12 years. Dusun believe a child of approximately 12 years and older can learn by the example of others.

Thus, Dusun "child care" ideally has four major stages: (1) In the first year of life most children are carefully watched and cared for by their mothers; (2) in the years from 2 to 7 children are protected and tended but given little formal instruction; (3) for children of 7 to 12 years of age, parents and other adults are supposed to make specific efforts to instruct children in ideal beliefs and ways of behavior; (4) after 12 years children are supposed to learn by following the example of others. The actual style of child care corresponds closely to this ideal, from an initial year of an intensive watchful care to a 5-year period of aiding the child to remain healthy and safe, to a 5-year period of relatively informal instruction with continuation of concern for protection from sickness and harm, to 5 years of minimal care and instruction until marriage or the age of 16.

The care of the 2- to 7-year-old child begins with a carry-over of typical infant care given by a mother in the first year of life and moves gradually to the activities

---

[1] The term *mèmurès* ("to instruct with words") is distinguished by Dusun from *mèmeràsu* ("to tell"), *mèmèsumèd* ("to give instruction"), and *pènèlele* ("to teach") as being appropriate usually in the first year of life.

A seven-year-old boy and an eight-year-old girl tend to their younger brothers.

comprising "minding" and "protecting." If a new baby has been born before a child is two years old, the older child is moved into the second phase of care quickly and without much attention by his parents to any consequences of the shift in the style of care. Between two and about four years a child usually is carried about in a sling on the back of an older brother or sister, or put down near his older sibling and not allowed to move about in play.

The responsibility for minding and protecting is given generally to the baby tender. Baby tenders usually take their responsibility seriously. Since the two-year-old is usually tended by the next oldest child, who may be only three or four years old, there is a continuation for the initial part of this time of a childhood version of a mother's activities with the infant; young baby tenders speak in tones of voice they think mothers use with infants and spend much of their time in their first months as child nurses in play at feeding, bathing, and singing to their charges. Since the baby tenders are burdened by the heavy weight of their charges, they tend to stay near the house talking and playing with neighborhood children also charged with the task of caring for their two- and three-year-old brothers and sisters. Baby tending is a responsibility of both sexes. A typical baby-tending group will have four to six nurses of both sexes. Occasionally a child of seven to ten years will be part of such a group. Usually older children responsible for baby tending will seek out each other's company because they feel it inappropriate to associate regularly with children not yet "the age of reason."

Older baby tenders do not usually try to continue the mother's style of care through the tone of voice and play imitative of feeding, bathing, and singing. Rather, these children engage in activities and play at games (see later discussion) felt by adults appropriate for children of this age. Then, the two- to four-year-old child is a participant in another type of childhood culture, typical of children of the "age of reason." A two- to four-year-old child's experiences in being tended by a three- to six-year-old sibling in a group of other three- to six-year-olds and their charges differ markedly from the experiences he will have in being tended by a seven- to ten-year-old sibling in groups of other seven- to ten-year-olds.

The child is exposed to and becomes part of a world where his older companions are treated differently by adults and act differently because they suppose them to be able to reason, understand, and learn properly. Long-term and regular observations of emotional and intellectual development of two- to four-year-old children tended by seven- to ten-year-olds or cared for by three- to six-year-olds tend to show what seem to be differences and evidences that these styles of care in Dusun enculturation could perhaps be important as one of the several possible *critical incidents* in development of Dusun personality.[2] The experiences of a two- to four-year-old in being cared for in a seven- to ten-year-old's world provide for situations which seem to set the stage for the young child to continue to easily identify and to exhibit approved behavior which is more complex and more adultlike. Nine of 13 Sensuron children of four to seven years who were second, third, and fourth children in their families and who were identified by adults other than parents in response to my question, "Which child under the age of seven already shows reason [*genaué*]?" had been regularly tended by a seven- to ten-year-old. This was also true in six of ten instances of four- to seven-year-olds in Baginda identified by adults as already possessing "reason."

Thus, along with the more obvious earlier *critical experiences* of birth, infant care, feeding, weaning, illness, accident, and the like, there are significant variations of experience in child care which Dusun children undergo which seem to promote development of personality functions and social skills. To the casual observer, Dusun parents seem to give almost no attention to the two- to four-year-old child. In the period from early morning until midafternoon of most days mothers and fathers are absent from the house and village working in the fields or jungle. Mothers usually carry their new infants with them, fully assigning the care of the two- to four-year-old to an older brother or sister. In the late afternoon and early evening the two- to four-year-old is still tended by his older sibling when he is not directly in contact with one of his parents. Observation of two- to four-year-old children in Sensuron

---

[2] The work of von Senden (1932), Lorenz (1952), Spitz (1946), and Piaget (1955) suggests that there are critical periods in the development of a child which are the times when he is most receptive to specific kinds of experiences. Their work has led to the "critical periods" hypothesis, which states that there are finite periods of limited duration in which certain experiences must take place if they are to become part of the child's repertoire of behavior responses; or there may be a period of increased efficiency for acquisition of experiences, before which such experience cannot be assimilated and after which the level of receptivity remains generally constant. I do not fully accept this hypothesis.

and Baginda provides estimates of data of time in contact with the baby tender, as compared to time in contact with one or both parents; on the average two- to four-year-old children spend more than 70 percent of every day in sole charge of and in contact with their child nurses. The remainder of the time of care was occupied in direct contacts with parents or parent surrogates as the children were alternately indulged, censored, frightened, or teased. Generally, the 30 percent or so of the time the two- to four-year-olds are interacting with their parents or parent surrogates is dominated by what at first seems to be an "indifferent" attitude of concern for the child, so long as he is healthy and safe from accident. In the first year of life parental concerns for the child are direct and continuing and are manifest in very different ways from the "indifferent" manner apparently shown toward the two- to four-year-old. However, the manner of concern manifested by parents toward the two- to four-year-old is not an accurate reflection of their basic emotional regard for the child. It is difficult for parents to give nearly all of their time to care of two children.

The two- to four-year-old is fed by his mother at meal times with other family members. He usually gets bathed when his child nurse takes a bath in the river. He is put down to defecate or urinate when his nurse performs these body functions. He sleeps in the carrying sling with his head lolling sideways or bobbing as his nurse plays or walks about. As he matures, he is allowed to walk about increasingly more of the time under the close control of his tender. In the second year of life a Dusun child walks little, is carried a lot, and is restricted to the carrying sling or the house floor or ground area near his parents or his child nurse. In the third year, a child spends increasingly more time walking alongside or behind his nurse in play and in moving about the village. Even by the early part of the fourth year, however, when the child is fully capable of independent movement and has many of his motor skills, he may be carried in the sling nearly 10 percent of every day unless by this time he has become the child nurse of a younger brother or sister.

In nuclear families (that is, families comprised of a mother, father, and their children) where there is no older child to be the child nurse, or in the instance of a firstborn child after its first year of life, the mother's or father's mother, and sometimes the father's father assume child-care tasks as parents go about the daily work of making a living. For this child the world is also very different than it would be if he were cared for by a three- to six-year-old child nurse, living in a three- to six-year-old's world of ideas and acts. The firstborn child is carried by his grandmother or grandfather into an adult world, where he is treated as part of the adult world by virtue of his being a "part" of the grandparent. From the carrying sling the child watches, hears, and sees adult activities and concerns most of every day, and the child is treated as more of an entity in himself by a grandparent than by any other person, including its parents. Grandparental nurses often carry on adult-level conversations with their two- to four-year-old charges, putting questions to them and providing retorts, explaining what is happening and giving reasons for their acts and the behavior of others. Grandparents, whether acting as baby tender for a two- to four-year-old or simply caring for any grandchild, conceive themselves to be governed by special events in time (see Williams 1965:13) which link grandparent and grandchild as a united entity in a firm emotional alliance of unique kin pairs comprised of alternate generations facing the intermediary, or parental, generation. A grandparent is the shield and bulwark in times of stress and trouble for a grandchild of any age; parents usually defer to their parents in instances where grandparents object to punishment or provide coddling and indulgence for be- havior, and most parents allow grandparents to directly alter instruction of older children.

The last-born child of a family is often tended by his mother in the age period of two to four rather than assigning him to an older sibling. When asked about this practice, one Sensuron mother said,

> They [the last-born] are all we have left of our children. So it is good to spend the years caring well for them. Then they will care for us when we are *nàkàgule* ["senile" or "returned to childhood"].

If a child is cared for by a grandparent in the time from two to four years of age, he is fed when the grandparent eats, bathes when he bathes, and is put down to eliminate when he eliminates. If the two- to four-year-old is the last-born and is cared for by its mother, the style of child care shifts very gradually from that usually given to the infant and to the two- to four-year-old. Last-born children sometimes are not weaned until they are well into their third year, and occasionally suckle at the breast until four or five years of age. Last-born children may be carried in the sling regularly and subjected to infant ritual growth verses, lullabies, and growth songs until they are three or four years old. For these children such experiences are also *critical incidents*; their extended period of infancy is in very marked contrast to the experiences to be found in three- to six-year-old and seven- to ten-year-old child-nurse culture, and the adult-world experiences provided by a grandparent nurse.

In summary, there are five variations of the "minding" and "protecting" style of care of the two- to four-year-old child: (1) *young child* (three- to six-year-old) nurses, (2) *older child* (seven- to ten-year-old) nurses, (3) *grandparental* or *"uncle- aunt"* nurses, (4) *extended infancy* care, and (5) *parental* care,

As noted, at about four to four-and-a-half years of age most Dusun children have gained the motor skills to enable them to readily move about independently of their child nurses. For most of their fourth year and part of their fifth year Dusun children are still closely supervised by their child nurses. By the middle of the fifth year the "minding" and "protecting" style of care ends, as the child becomes either a young child nurse or part of an independent play group (that is, without child nurses) comprised of other unsupervised children between five and seven or eight years of age. These groups of five- to seven-year-olds move about the area of the neighborhood and play independently of the two social groups formed by young child nurses and older child nurses. There were usually about eight such play groups in Sensuron and four in Baginda village. The play and activities of children in these groups is described later (see the section "Children's Activities"). There are no formal decisions made by parents about ending the supervision of the child nurse of their now very mobile young charge. The termination of the "mind- ing" and "protecting" style of care is gradual, taking place over at least a half year, if the child has not become a child nurse himself. For the children assigned the tasks of a child nurse while they are between four and five years of age, the end of their own "minding-protecting" care is at the time they first pick up their young charge in the carrying sling; then the "watched" becomes the "watcher" and is expected to be responsible for the two-year-old handed him, as others were responsible for him.

For the four- to seven-year-old who does not become a child nurse, the days are composed of long hours of general freedom from close parental or nurse supervision. However, the play groups tend to stay close to houses, or play in houses and on house porches where a grandparent or other adult is present during the day. The four- to seven-year-olds in the freely moving play groups (those, for example, not supervised by child nurses) in Sensuron and Baginda village are never very far away from an old man sitting on a house porch cutting out a tool, or an old woman preparing food or making some domestic implement. While the adults present in the villages appear to take little notice of the nonsupervised four- to seven-year-olds, the children of these play groups seem well aware of the locations of adults and tend to cluster in the areas near houses where an adult is present. On the days when adults are absent from houses where they usually are present, these play groups move near other houses where there are adults working or resting.

Between 7 and 12 years of age children are expected to care fully for themselves in all matters of feeding, bathing, and elimination. In this time there is a different type of care by parents, a care which has as its main focus of concern insuring that a child learns by direct and formal instruction, or *pènèlele,* which is given by responsible and knowledgeable adults. The period from seven to nine years of age is one of some stress for many children, for they find themselves again under regular and close supervision by adults, who are seeking to make them remember and to repeat back the things they are supposed to learn. In the time from two to four years of age, as the charge of a child nurse or a grandparent nurse, children are rarely addressed, asked for an opinion, or made a real part of the play group of the child nurses. When the child becomes a nurse or joins a four- to seven-year-old play group, he continues to exist in a child's world and does not have to deal with demands that he know or act in "proper" ways.

During their seventh and eighth years, however, Dusun children are rapidly brought into the sphere of activities and influence of their parents and parent-surrogates (father's and mother's brothers and sisters and mothers and fathers) and are made to understand that they are expected to be serious concerning life and the world they must live in as adults. At this age, children begin to occasionally accompany their same-sexed parent, grandparent, or a mother's or father's brother or sister during some daily work tasks. Some boys of 7 and 8 take the family water buffalo to the grazing areas in the early morning and return them in the afternoon to the village. They may sometimes accompany their father, grandfathers, uncles, or much older brothers in these tasks. Girls of 7 to 8 begin to sometimes help their mothers, grandmothers, aunts, or much older sisters in gathering and preparing foods for the daily meals. Boys of this age often are told to sit and watch and later asked to participate in the making of agricultural and hunting tools. They are sometimes put to doing light work in the rice fields. Girls of 7 and 8 years are told to remain alongside their mothers or other female relatives to watch and later to help in domestic chores. By 10 to 12 years of age some Dusun children are occupied in work activities which can consume much of their time. Most do not work at regular tasks until puberty. Chores are directly contributory to the welfare of the nuclear family and are supposed to be done as adult-type work. Adults do not make the 7- to 12-year-old child "practice" at tasks which are imitations of adult activities. Children of this age begin watching adults engage in adult tasks and then are instructed formally in ways to perform these tasks; they are instructed as well on many other matters of concern to adults, such as ritual and fortune, disease, aggression, and so on.

Children of 10 to 12 years of age who do their new work tasks well and easily have adults say proudly of them to other adults, "He understands how to help his parents in all their work!" This is ideally said of boys of this age who can (1) "feed and care for water buffalo," (2) "help plow a rice field," or (3) "assist in repairing at a house building." Girls who can (1) "pound and sift rice," (2) "cook rice and vegetables," (3) "carry wood and water," (4) "wash utensils used in cooking," (5) "gather jungle foods," and (6) "sew and weave" are said to merit such praise. A child of 10 to 12 who is slow to learn these ideal ways is termed a "child without reason." A slow learner is said to be naturally that way if one of his four grandparents was reputed to be slow or dull witted; most often the responsibility for a dull child is laid to the father's *teŋran* "because the mother's *teŋran* is more responsible for the child's body than for his reason." The explanation given for the child's slowness because of an inheritance of stupidity was expressed in the comment of a Sensuron woman when she said of a 6-year-old boy, "He is a slow learner because of his grandfather." Dusun also recognize that some children of 7 to 12 years learn rapidly and well, despite the fact that both parents are known to be "stupid." In such cases, the child's capacity to learn well is ascribed to the brilliance of a male grandparent. Adults say of such a child, "He learns well because of the other generation."

The 7- to 12-year-old child receives a part of his care and his direct instruction in work tasks from his father's younger brothers and sisters. These persons are somewhat more affectionate and familiar than mother's younger brothers and sisters, although this depends on the location of the houses of these relatives in a community. A father's brother teases and plays with his young male nephews, urging them to play tricks on their father's sisters; between 7 and 12 years, boys are regularly put up to teasing father's sisters by calling out stylized expressions such as, "Our aunt cannot chase us because she is weak!" while they run away from her in mock horror and fright. Father's sisters encourage girls between 7 and 12 to the teasing of father's brothers in a similar manner. Children of this age sometimes learn much of their specific work knowledge from these particular relatives. Grandparents give very little work-task instruction during these years of childhood. Usually children of 7 to 12 learn details of manners, morality, specific and complex knowledge (distance, depth and time measures, a system of numbers, and so on) from grandparents of the same sex.

Thus care in this later period of childhood shifts to a close supervision by parents and parent-surrogates of a child's learning about adult activities. During the period of time from 7 to 12 years children are watched regularly and disciplined for failures to perform as expected. This is in marked contrast to the preceding years, in which the things a child is expected to know or learn are generally ignored.

As noted previously, adults believe that after 12 years of age a child must learn by following the example of others and by listening to adults discuss matters of belief and action. Child care between 12 and 15 or 16 years of age shifts back to a style somewhat similar to the care given members of 5- to 7-year-old play groups; the 12- to 13-year-old is instructed less regularly in his work tasks by parents and is expected to just do a satisfactory job. Since he has been caring for his personal needs for many years, the 12- or 13-year-old is not bothered by parents or other adults about his elimination, bathing, or eating habits unless they grossly violate adult ideal beliefs. Then the child is openly scolded by a parent for "being like a little child." Otherwise children nearing adolescence have little formal attention or comment given to them by adults. It should also be said that in the normal course of events Dusun parents worry very little about problems of adolescence.

Most Dusun parents make few special efforts to protect the young child from physical harm by accidents with knives, spears, poison blowgun darts, burns from falling into fires or knocking over a pot of boiling water, being bitten or harmed by animals or getting caught up in flooded streams. Child care (including "minding" and "protecting") is oriented toward the dangers of the harmful supernatural and human beings seeking to destroy health and alter good fortune. Dusun parents will only occasionally rush to pick up a child in the way of two large male water buffalo about to fight, or hang up out of reach large bush knives with razor-sharp blades. However, parents will dash immediately into the house yard when the sun begins to shine through a lightly falling rain and a rainbow arches over the horizon, for this is the time of *àra tadau,* when the fearful *pàmàèbiè* comes to capture souls. Dusun child care centers upon protecting children from dangers felt to be real by Dusun and not upon the hazards perceived by persons from another culture.

It was startling to us to see a two-year-old chopping at a stick of bamboo with a knife with an edge so sharp his father later shaved with the blade. We were taken aback by seeing toddlers carrying snakes and stinging insects about and throwing them away. However, parents of these children and other adults were not often concerned at such activities. As *dao* of Sensuron put the matter, "Children never get hurt from these things anyhow. And if they do they get over it. They do not get over the disease givers or spirits of the dead eating their souls. Or someone trying to steal their luck. So I worry about the things I need to worry about."

CHILDREN'S ACTIVITIES

The product of one research technique will be used here to briefly summarize and describe the general nature of children's daily activities by providing a sample of diary notes from daily field observations.

The following chronological sequence record (see Chapter 2) was made as I watched and listened to the activities about the houses of our Sensuron primary social unit; all the events noted took place within 30 yards and most occurred within 10 to 15 yards of my location:

Low Mist: 63°F. TRW (Diary of Events) 21 April 60 Thurs. Sen. P. 1/4

6:15 A.M.—*àndak* (adult male, house 149) comes to the front porch of *gudol* (adult male, house 3) and calls; *gudol* comes on porch. They talk about going hunting. *loloŋ* (male, 6 years, house 3) comes out of the house, stands beside father, squats beside him, gets up, wraps leg about porch post, squats again, repeatedly flips hands, palms down, then up. *bàlàtak* (adult female, house 3) comes onto porch carrying new baby (male, 19 days) in sling, tells *loloŋ* to go to river with water carriers and bring home water. When he ignores her, she pushes him over from his squat with her right foot, then reaches down and raps him on top of head with knuckles of her right hand, while shouting at him, "Go now, you lazy boy!" The two men ignore this; *bàlàtak* shifts baby from her back, gives him her left breast to nurse and stands, hands at her side, listening to two men discuss location of their hunt for the day.

6:20 A.M.—*hili* (male, 6 years, house 5) comes on the porch of house 5, empties water from bamboo carrier onto one hand, then the other, takes a drink, gargles loudly, spits water over porch edge, rubs hands over top of head, goes back in house, comes back out, followed by *tengai* (adult female, house 5), carrying new baby (female, 26 days) in sling. She squats and begins to wash out a rice pot. While she works, pouring water in and scrubbing inside with her right hand, she calls out to *làhim* (adult female, house 4) and they carry on a conversation on plans for making rice wine for a party two weeks ahead. *hili* runs over to near porch of house 3, listens to *gudol* and *ànduk* talk. The other children of house 3 are now in yard playing. *maine* (female, 5 years) has *tadi* (male, 2½ years) in sling on her back, and *likà* (female, 10 years) is carrying her cousin *amini* (male, 4 years) in a sling. *likà* pinches *hili* on the right buttock (he has only a shirt on). He chases her about the house, with *maine* following, trying to pinch him again. This goes on for five minutes, with the three running hard about the house, laughing and shouting, *"hoi! hoi!"* The adults ignore them.

6:30 A.M.—*làhim* comes out of house 4, stands beside steps, pulls up skirt to her knees, spreads her feet, urinates while continuing her conversation with *tengai* on making rice wine for party. *làhim* has *ubinà* (female, 1 year) in sling on her back. *maroksin* (adult male, house 6) and *ogàk* (adult male, house 8) are squatted down in front of house 8; *maroksin* is cutting *ogàk's* hair with a small knife. *sautin* (female, 7 years) and *bili* (male, 5 years), children of *ogàk*, sit on ground and watch haircutting.

6:40 to 7:00 A.M.—I am interrupted by *sàndau* (adult male, house 11), who has a small wound on his right thigh from accident with a knife; it has stopped bleeding, so I apply medication and then dress wound, give him oral antibiotic, and tell him to return at 5:00 P.M.

7:00 A.M.—*bàlàtak* is sitting on porch of house 3, with new male baby in her lap, nursing at the left breast. *likà* is combing and picking lice from *bàlàtak's* hair. *noelà* (female, 2½ years) grabs comb from *likà*, throws it off porch. *likà* pinches her very hard on the arm, retrieves comb, while shouting, "Stupid little girl!" at her; *noelà* runs into the house, screaming. I can see her through open door throw a water carrier against far house wall.

7:05 A.M.—*suŋean* (adult female, house 9) is sitting on fallen coconut tree trunk in front of her house, shredding tobacco leaves. She is talking with *làhïm* (adult female, house 4) about the first fight which occurred at a party last week in house 111; *làhïm* is carrying a number of pieces of tapioca root. *gàtoliḳ* (male, house 9, 10 years) comes out of house, throws three puppies onto ground. They land flat, get up, staggering. *mari* (female, 6 years) comes out of house 9 after *gàtoliḳ*, carrying *ustin* (male, 18 months) on her back in sling. She picks up one of the puppies, then holds it so *ustin* can see it. *ustin* nuzzles at dog's nose. *mari* then throws dog away flat onto the ground and goes off down main path. *làhïm* stands shifting from one foot to another, scratches herself, then squats down, shifting finally to a seated position.

7:10 A.M.—four boys (*heḳol*, 8 years, house 6; *paris*, 10 years, house 12; *nànïŋ*, 10 years, house 14; and *loïŋàn*, 9 years, house 2) walk to area in front of house 9, pick up large stones, begin throwing them: *heḳol* scratches a line on the ground with a piece of bamboo, stands on it, then throws a stone by pushing it upward with a shot-put-like motion. He steps aside; *loïŋàn*, then *paris*, and then *nànïŋ*, step up and follow. Then they measure off the distance the stones are thrown by pacing from line. *nànïŋ* has thrown his stone farther than others. He scratches a line on ground with a stick at this point, then throws his stone back in other direction. The other boys, in the order of *heḳol, paris,* and *loïŋàn* take turns (their order corresponds apparently to distance achieved). The game proceeds, as stones are thrown back in other direction, then back again.

7:20 A.M.—*aulip* (male, 15 years, house 9) joins group, takes stone from *heḳol*, throws with great deliberation and flexing of muscles, to obvious admiration of 4 boys. They watch as he throws, paces off distance, and throws back and forth again five times. He leaves, going into house 4, and boys begin to imitate his actions in throwing.

7:25 A.M.—*dao* (adult male, house 9) comes by, stops, tells me he is off to hunt pigs near his garden. He shows me his spear tip, which has been newly sharpened. He calls his dogs with the familiar, *"ahela! ahela!"* and goes off up the main path. *gèndarid* (adult male, house 14) goes by carrying a piece of large-diameter bamboo some 20 feet long on his shoulder, and with *intaŋ* (male, 2½ years) in sling on his back, while *uanis* (male, 9 years) walks behind him with a smaller diameter piece of bamboo about 6 feet long on his shoulder.

7:30 A.M.—*bàlàtaḳ* (adult female, house 3) is now standing by house sifting rice in split bamboo tray. She has new child in sling, covered with an old skirt. *ḳïntunà* (female, 6 years, house 13) and *gontriḳ* (female, 4 years, house 17) are in branches of tree just behind *bàlàtaḳ,* bouncing up and down in time to the rice-sifting rhythm; they begin to sing the verses of the *sesïndeun* song which has often been sung by 5–7-year-olds in the last month after the harvest ("I am looking at the party. All of us must die, so enjoy yourselves. See, if you are dead, you cannot come back to the party!")

7:35 A.M.—as *bàlàtaḳ* continues to work, the two girls climb down from tree, still singing, and begin to dance; the shoulders are rotated slowly in the opposite direction from the hips, while the feet are advanced in a dragging shuffle, right foot first. The head is erect, with body weight slightly forward and down into pelvic basin as the body is bobbed at the knees; arms are held out from the sides, at shoulder level, fingers spread and upward. As the two girls dance, their voices change to the husky, crackling tones used in alternation with the high soprano in love songs, and in songs of war.

7:45 A.M.—*sàdekàn* (adult male, house 14) comes by, stops and sits down and begins to talk about the court hearing set for that afternoon for the settlement of o's supposed attempts to kill g by poison and through ritual. (See notes, this date 7:45 A.M. to 7:55 A.M. on detail of dispute.)

For Dusun children play often consists of games, the singing of songs, the telling of riddles and jokes, and stylized teasing and taunting. Games involve play alone and in groups and use of playthings made of stone, bamboo, rattan, discarded water-buffalo horns, soft clay figures, and domestic tools used as toys. Children under four years usually play with objects used about the house, or with pieces of wood and bamboo picked up from the house yard. Much of the use of household items involves filling, pouring, and piling up of dirt or the carrying of rainwater to splash into another puddle. Sticks are used to dig holes in the ground and to dig ditches to carry water from a mud puddle to a hole or to another puddle. Children between two and four years also spend time at games involving throwing, breaking, hitting, and picking over objects and piles of objects. Most of these games can be played alone or as part of a group. Typically, these are the games of young child nurses when they play together. Since this play involves being in the dirt, mud, and water and use of the body, hands, and feet as playthings, children of two to four usually get dirty early in the day and remain so most of every day.

Children of four to seven years continue this type of play in a more elaborate manner in the play groups. There is more play of a "house" or "family activity" type in which games are made of adult work tasks and activities, including sexual behavior. The playthings used by the two- to four-year-olds are employed by four- to seven-year-olds to make scenes of cultivation or depict the gathering of foods or care of animals and to set locations for imaginary play in the settling of disputes, making war, or dealing with major family events such as ritual celebrations and trips to visit relatives and friends in other villages. Most of the games of four- to seven-year-olds are simply more elaborate and planned filling, pouring, piling of dirt, splashing, carrying, and leading about of rainwater, and more systematic piling and knocking about of objects. Also, four- to seven-year-olds are much more systematic in destruction of objects, such as sticks and rattan, than are two- to four-year-olds. The amount of time which involves the careful construction of dioramas or play replicas of fields and adult work tasks comprises less than 10 percent of the game time of a child of this age group.

The making and use of playthings in a more systematic manner, such as molding soft clay animals, or constructing a duplicate of a rice-field irrigation system, are secondary to the imaginary conversations carried on aloud in solitary and group play situations. Dusun children of four to seven years of age seem more concerned with acting out the verbal rather than the physical aspects of the situations they play at creating. Their scenes made in play are simple stages onto which they project much more elaborate imaginary verbal events. Typically a group of four- to seven-year-olds spend a few moments in play construction of a scene, then an hour talking and acting the roles of the adults they imagine themselves to be in play.

Children of two to seven years also play at being "victims and aggressors"; group play may shift quickly to piles of children struggling in a muddy hole or to individuals pushing down other children, then running about in circles in a limited space, screaming loudly, until caught and tripped or hit by the other child, with both wriggling onto the ground again, then repeating the game once more. The four- to seven-year-olds spend less time in piles of bodies, with thrashing masses of children rolling about on the ground, and more time pushing each other down from a seated position, then chasing each other over a larger area, waving sticks or flailing about with a piece of rattan. The screams and verbal content of these games are said by children to portray a play scene of being attacked by an enemy, then the chase and a final victory over the attacker.

The play of falling into groups of children in which there is close touch contact between bodies is a continuation of the earlier regular contacts involved in care in a carrying sling and is further reflected in the fact that four- to seven-year-olds often carry each other about piggyback and play at several games in which one child must carry another one astride his back in order to compete; the favorite game of this type appears to be a form of "horse and rider," which involves the children milling about and bumping into each other until the whole group, often of ten or more, fall in a heap.

The play of 7- to 12-year-olds shifts away from being in the dirt and using simple playthings to organized game activities using elaborate actions and playthings. There is a rapid diminution of close body-contact play, as parents enforce sex distinctions and belief about "proper activities"; where 4- to 7-year-olds play freely in groups mixing the sexes, 7- to 12-year-olds segregate themselves into same-sex play groups most of the time.

Typically, the organized games of 7- to 12-year-olds involve between four and ten children organized into "sides" or "teams" which compete against each other. A few games involving individual competition (see diary notes, given previously) are played, but the majority of 7- to 12-year-old games are based on activities of individuals as part of a temporary social group. A description of two games played cooperatively by 7- to 12-year-olds will illustrate the nature of such play. The game of *pàtàm* involves lines in a rectangular shape being drawn on the ground with a stick, enclosing an area about 5 by 10 feet. In the center of the space a shallow hole, about 6 inches in diameter and about 3 inches deep, is dug with the tip of a stick. Sides among the boys or girls of a play group are usually chosen by the older children, who call out the names of their "side" until there are four to six chosen in each group. Each participant seeks out and brings to the game two small, flat stones about 2 inches in diameter. The game begins by a child lobbing his stones at the hole in the center of the rectangle, attempting to place them in the opening. A second player, from the second "side," then tries to strike these stones with his own stones in such a manner as to knock them outside the bounds of the rectangle area. The third child, from the first side, then steps up and tries to strike the second child's stones from the rectangle; he is followed by a player from the second side again, and so on, until everyone has had one opportunity to throw their stones. If a player strikes both stones from the rectangle, his side wins the game. If the stones of the first player are not struck from the rectangle, his side wins, and the leader of the opposing side then leads off another game by throwing his two stones at the hole in the rectangle. If both the stones thrown lodge and remain in the hole, the side represented by the player wins. There is no "score" which determines final victory in the game. Play proceeds until the children are bored or distracted by other events.

A second game often played by 7- to 12-year-olds is termed "to catch in the basket" and consists of two sides of four children each taking turns "invading" and "defending" a territory marked out by lines drawn on the ground with a pointed stick. A square of about 30 or 40 feet on each side is divided into four equal sections by drawing lines through the center, then across the center of the square. One child from a side of four children "guards" or "protects" each of the sections of the square while the children of the opposite side attempt to run through the sections to the other side without being tapped by both hands of the defenders. The object of the game is to attempt to have all four "offense" players get through the sections without being tagged. It is permissible in the game to send all four players into one section at one time; the only rule of procedure which must be followed is that the "attacker" must slap his right palm into the right palm of the "defender" before being eligible to try to run the square. When all four players ("attackers") get through the squares untouched, the sides change, with the defenders going on the attack and vice versa. It is characteristic that the game is played with vigor and that participants often send each other sprawling with their "taps."

Other games played by 4- to 7-year-olds include versions of "hopscotch," "rounders," and "hide-and-go-seek," and there are many variations on the game themes termed "high jumping," "long jumping," or "racing" to determine which contestant is the strongest or fastest. There are also many variations of the games of "fighting" and "madness," which involve hitting at others with sticks in mock combat or in play at the hysteria of mental illness. There are a number of games involving objects which participants use to demonstrate that their skills or strength are greater than others playing on an opposing side. Carved wooden tops of a variety of sizes, small windmills, and windvanes of sago and coconut palm leaves and carved wood "propellers," some up to 4 feet in length, are used in game competition. Stilts made of bamboo, ranging in size from 3 to 7 feet long, are used in a version of the "horse and rider" game where participants seek to throw each other off balance with shoves administered by arms or sticks. A game form played in Sensuron and not seen in Baginda involves a "war with words" between the 7- to 12-year-olds of the two dialect divisions of the village. Two groups of 10 to 20 boys, or girls, gather beside a large slab of rock, raised some 60 years before the present to symbolize the end of head taking in the immediate area of the community, and "go against each other" with ritual and stylized shouted insults, jibes and teasing concerning the "funny" speech of each dialect, the stupidity of grandparents, and the relative ugliness of girls (or boys) from the two dialect groups and the reputations of dialect

Boys of six to eight years sliding down a steep muddy hill slope on bamboo "sleds."

group members for greed, stinginess, cowardice, theft, and sexual misbehavior. This "game" vastly amuses adult onlookers and usually ends with a mud fight, after which everyone bathes in the river.

Other games of 7 to 12-year-olds include a variety of water tag played in the river at the village bathing place and fighting with discarded water-buffalo horns on the ends of bamboo poles in an imitation of fights which occur between male buffalo. Also, there are a number of games involving sliding or rolling downhill using bamboo "sleds" to slip on a muddy and rain dampened slope; a half piece of large diameter bamboo about 10 to 20 feet long is often used as a "toboggan" by four or five children to go down a hillside, and a raftlike structure is built of bamboo sticks, 3 inches wide and about 4 to 6 feet long, which are woven together by forcing them over and under each other to create a platform. The platform is placed on top of four or five large-diameter bamboo pieces about 6 feet long. Then, several children sit on the platform while others tilt them over the hill slope, sending them rolling headlong down the incline on the bamboo rollers to end in a laughing, tangled mass of bodies as the platform careens from the last bamboo roller.

Most of the more than 20 games of 7- to 12-year-olds are played by both boys and girls. Most games involve pulling, pushing, striking, hitting, close body contact, and much noise, accompanied by loud and raucous comments, lending the impression that this play is a part of the Dusun *milieu* of restless and vigorous activity and forceful expression of developing dominant personality needs.

One of the characteristic sounds of village life is children singing at play. Adult and children's songs comprise more than 50 commonly known verse and melody forms. These are differentiated from songs of lovers, wedding-day songs, and songs sung at parties and at times of ritual feasting. The songs of lovers and wedding and party songs comprise a group of more than 30 widely known and sung melodies and verses. The songs of 4- to 7-year-olds are composed of simple verses with extensive use of nonsense terms. Some examples of songs of 4- to 6-year-olds follow:

> There they are _____
> riding on toys!
>
> There they are _____
> looking down the hill, down the hill!
>
> There is *pièn,*
> pretending to die.
>
> *rusa* has given birth,
> *imelun* is the father;
> who will take that baby
> that belongs to no family;
> my small jackfruit?[3]

Children of 7 to 12 years sing more complex songs, with detailed verses and more involved melodies. Such songs are often sung in harmony:

> "An old jar broke," the boy said,
> "When it dropped on my head like
> that harmful caterpillar."
> "It was hanging down like a vegetable,"
> said the boy!
>
> *sebdàne* is afraid to go down there,
> to meet death in *sàntàne's* house!
>
> I curse at the *ƙutau* bird
> who flys obscenely by wiggling
> his waist!
>
> Be kind, fair, true my friend,
> and not like the insect
> which sucks blood from me.

Older children often sing adult songs as they play. Some examples are:

---

[3] The topic of language acquisition by Dusun children will be reported upon in a forthcoming paper on the subject.

You wish to go home sister.
Do not go home over the hills.
Walk the easy way, where the
fruit clusters for you to eat
on the way.
I invite you, sister, to come
this way.

There is a heavy rain downstream.
There is a well-turned hairknot
at the back of my jackfruit's head.
I would marry her, but she
refuses because I have no dowry
to give to her!

Children sing as they walk or play in groups or sit in solitary play. The tunes are distinctive and are usually sung with an application of skill and taste following Dusun beliefs of the "good" and "beautiful" in musical expression. Children capable of singing a "lovely" song are complimented by adults for their possession of reason. Songs are also used by children as forms of aggression:

Having children,
in the land of the Brunei,
three clustered as on
a coconut tree!

This is a derisive song about Moslems, who are supposed to have their children in bunches, as twins or triplets. Another aggressive song form is:

There is a stranger eating feces!
Hear the dog bark!
Oh, it is only *gànalis* [name of person]!

Dusun children also learn and often use a great many riddles as part of their play and other activities. Riddling behavior is not used by adults for amusement, although merriment may accompany the giving and answering of a riddle. Riddles serve the functions of channeling social conflicts, reducing interpersonal aggression, teaching rules of social action, validating the Dusun system of culture, explaining the world, as a form of magic, as a conceptualizing mechanism for exploring new ideas, and integrating the social system. A detailed discussion with 188 examples of Dusun riddles which have been collected has been published elsewhere (Williams 1963a). Children's riddles tend to be less complex than those given by adults, but do serve the same general functions, as well as the function of making new ideas available in a form which can easily be remembered by a child. Some examples of children's riddles are:

Four-year-old male: It is alive, yet it wants to bury itself in the earth.
    Answer: A rat.

Eight-year-old female: He who carries will be rotten before the load.
    Answer: A bamboo water carrier.

Twelve-year-old male: You can carry one basket, but you cannot carry two.
Answer: To defecate in a hurry.

Children's jokes sometimes take the form of stylized sayings, such as the one noted previously in the teasing comment of a boy to his mother's or father's sisters. More often, jokes are expressed in the form of gestures or body postures which denote teasing or obscene comment. Thus, a boy or girl of 7 to 12 years will tease a father's or mother's sister or brother by holding up his right leg, bent back at the knee and supported by the right hand under the ankle, while hopping about unsteadily on the other leg. This teasing gesture is widely understood to mean, "Although I have only one leg, you are so weak and old you cannot catch me!" Younger adult relatives usually respond to the gesture by running after the child and pinching him sharply on the ear while commenting on the child's lack of respect for his betters. Obscene gestures, usually denoting some form of sexual intercourse, are used by children to respond to the aggression of other children or adults. The gestures used are the forms commonly employed by adults and comprise more than 15 specific acts involving hand, face, and total body movements.

Children's games, songs, riddles, and jokes, all comprise a vital part of the enculturation experience in Dusun society. These aspects of childhood provide opportunity for a child to learn some of the important content of his culture and to practice at social relations with others in ways in which he must learn to submit his own personality needs to long-term control and specific forms of expression in order to be a part of the variety of social groups typical of Dusun life.

STATUS OF CHILDREN

Dusun parents judge the maturation of children from two years to puberty through use of a series of clearly defined status terms. These terms generally serve as indicators of the behavior supposed to be exhibited by a child. The newborn infant is termed *nàsusu* ("newly born"), while the infant of one month to one year of age is described as *baràgàŋ* ("red-faced baby"). From the age of one year, or the time of walking with assistance, to the fifth birthday, the descriptive terms *kèndu* ("boy"), *uogè* ("girl") and *oiè, àgàŋ,* and *àsàn* ("boy" or "girl") are used as status markers.[4] Girls from two to five years are described as *iŋà nè tàpe* ("without a skirt"). Boys of this age are termed *iŋà nè sàntud* ("without a loincloth"). From five years to adolescence, both boys and girls are described as *tànàk* ("child"). From seven or eight years of age until marriage boys are termed as *tànàk uàgu* ("child man") while girls are called *sumàndàk* ("virgin"). A physically adult boy or girl not yet married but behaving sometimes as an adult is described as *nàsukèd* ("new man") or *kèsusunè* ("she has breasts"). A physically adult boy not married and generally behaving as an adult is called *tolunlied* ("already a man"). The collective term

---

[4] As a special mark of affection for a child, parents or other adults call a girl of two to five years *kèndu* ("boy") and boys of this age *uogè* ("girl"). It is often a mark of a parent's concern and unhappiness with a two- to five-year-old's behavior when they address the child with the "proper" sex status designation.

used by parents to describe all their children is *sàkàg*. The general condition of childhood, or "boyhood" and "girlhood," which is believed to exist from two years until puberty, is described by use of the term *kàtànàkun*. The period and general condition of adolescence, from puberty to marriage, is described as *minsusukèd*. There are more than ten other status terms of maturation and behavior development (for example, *tànàk e gulu*—"oldest son or daughter"; *tànàk dè kàrèpè*—"child too small to strike with the fingers"; *iŋà mèlehiŋ*—"orphan"; *tànàk nàmpàŋ*—"illegitimate child").

The status terms used before five years of age generally are indicators of physical development. After five years, or from the time of first use of the term *tànàk* to describe a child, status terms denote both maturation and exhibition of expected or "proper" behavior. Adults will not describe a child as *tànàk uàgu* or *sumàndàk* if they still behave as a *tànàk*, although they may be undergoing puberty. The behavior skills expected by parents of a five-year-old, or *tànàk*, vary within a range of Dusun expectations of what is "proper" behavior. Usually five- and six-year-olds are told to "act like a *tànàk*" when parents notice the presence or exhibition of a certain mixture of physical and behavior signs. Among these signs are the skill of walking frontwards down a house ladder while alternating feet in the descent, the ability to hop about, alternating feet, the ability to correctly carry out errands outside of the home, an exhibition of some skill in the use of common domestic tools (especially a knife for a boy and a rice pounding stick for girls), some inquiry by the child about the meaning of ritual, political, and economic activities, the overhand throwing of small objects, knowledge of the time divisions of day and night, differentiation of and regular use of one hand over the other, and an ability to carry at least half the weight carried by an adolescent.

The names given to children also are status markers. Dusun only give names to their children and to "the two animals always with man—his dog and his water buffalo." Names are not given regularly to objects or possessions. Dusun parents do not usually give names to children under two years of age. One mother said, "If I give the *baràgàŋ* a name and he dies, then we have lost him." Between the age of two to three years, children are named according to the way the child acts, appears, or speaks, or because of a parent's wish to use a name of a close friend, usually someone living in another community, whose name is "pleasing to hear and say." These names may be retained by a child through his adult life and are used by him to identify himself. Names are not traded or bartered, and are rarely altered, once given by parents. Three women in Sensuron and Baginda are called *letà*, from the sound *tàtà* made by adults as they teach a child to walk; when these persons repeated the sounds, they were named for their utterances. A common adult male name is *gàhoie* or "thin" from body appearance as a two- to three-year-old. The names *làmpàs* ("slender faced, long legs"), and *lèmbegit* ("holding on tightly") are not unusual in Dusun society. Other names deriving from some peculiar act or appearances of a two- to three-year-old include *lèdtit* ("belly sticking out"), *gutèŋ* ("stinking"), *èrubès* ("loose bowels"), *karèp* ("burnt rice at the bottom of a pot") and *korèp* ("ears pulled close to the head"). Some adults have no name and go through life being called *baràgàŋ* ("red-faced baby") without apparent embarrassment at the lack of a personal designation. This is related to the fact that Dusun believe it is "unkind" (that is, "improper") to use a personal name in addressing a relative or friend. It is believed "better" to employ specific kin terms addressing another person than to use a personal name. On occasion, if the person being addressed is not liked or not friendly, status terms (such as *tànàk uàgu; kosai*—"male"; *tàndu*—"female") are used. Thus, it is possible for a Dusun to spend much of his life without ever hearing his "name" spoken. As they go about their affairs, Dusun are usually addressed by kinship terms and reply in kin terms. Even when being addressed in a taunt, derision, or an argument, status terms rather than names will usually be used. Names are most often employed in third-person reference in a conversation between two persons concerning someone who is not a relative or special friend or does not hold a special position in the community (for example, male ritual specialist) and can be referred to by a well-known designation.

FOOD AND CLEANLINESS TRAINING

The Dusun term hunger as *losun*. They say that children and adolescents are "naturally hungry." Adults look for signs of hunger as one indication of children's health and growth. It is believed that persons recovering from a critical illness are restored to health through a great natural hunger which impels them to eat to regain health. When adults become unusually hungry in a time of an abundance of food, they are said to be "possessed" by "something" which urges or causes the food greed. It is generally believed that a special form of a soul of the dead (*ràgun*), termed *muminsuo,* has taken possession of a victim's body by trickery. The trickery is described in the comment of *gèndarìd* of Sensuron:

Children watch as a dead pig has its hair singed off over a fire. The pig has been killed after use in a ritual to "cool" off the sickness afflicting an elderly man.

That one [ràgun] goes and shakes a fruit tree owned by someone, then gets hit on the head by the fruit as it falls. Then he screams in pain and says, "Now I can go eat the human being who owns this tree!" Sometimes they trip themselves and then blame it on someone.

It is common that Dusun will attempt to trick the trickster spirit to protect themselves. After cutting down a jungle tree they place a stone on the stump to mislead the ràgun into believing that the stone cut the tree. If the trick fails, the ràgun is believed to seek out the person who has attempted to fool him, take possession, and to begin to eat away at the victim's body.

When a person is "possessed" and it is believed that he is destined to die because he is at the limit of his naturally allotted fate (Williams 1965:Chapter 4), there is usually no attempt to cure or save him. If divination shows that the possessed person has not reached the limit of his personal luck, it is believed possible to have a female ritual specialist "make good and eliminate an offense" by substitution of a fowl or pig for the ràgun to eat; souls of the dead are believed to like fowl, pig, and water buffalo as food even more than humans.

A child or adolescent who manifests hunger beyond "natural hunger" is said to be possessed by a ràgun. The special expression "There is a dog in the stomach" denotes this condition. A child afflicted with such a condition is subjected to the same style of divination and ritual cure used for adults. Parents pay special attention to whether children and adolescents are "satisfied" when they have eaten. Parents caution children with a special expression to eat slowly to take advantage of the health in food, and children are reminded after they complete a meal to use the proper expression denoting they are "satisfied" with the meal: "I am satisfied." Children sometimes use the adult joking expression of "a jar full" to answer the parent's query on completion of a meal, or reply with the polite expression "The jar spills over." Children are expected to learn to greet an ill friend on a visit to his house with the expression "Take some food to get well," and they are expected to learn at the ages of between five and seven years that when a person refuses food offered by a host he causes bad luck to the host and himself since refusal of food is a sign of impending death.

As noted earlier, parents believe there is a specific relationship between food and body fat and between fat and growth. At meal times parents regularly say to children, "Take the food and soon you will grow," or "Take the food and your calves will be big." Children say they want "fat calves" for it is believed these are the sign of a strong person.

Dusun adults are concerned with the effects on children of famine or a time of food shortage caused by crop failure. Many Dusun families regularly experience a short supply of rice in the several months just before harvest. Then, parents borrow rice at high rates of interest to insure their children have enough to satisfy their "natural" condition of hunger. In some families a very small amount of rice is mixed in with large amounts of yams, tapioca, or bananas to feed children during the "short supply" of food. During shortages of food, children are constantly reminded of the value of rice and other foods for health, work, fortune, and life. Children learn that the general term for food, pàḳànàn, means "rice," and that the term for rice, pari, means "food." To avoid offending the "rice spirit" children are warned by parents not to waste food by spilling it or throwing it away. Parents will say in a sharp voice, "Don't offend the rice spirit!" when a child drops rice on the house floor or leaves an amount uneaten. To teach the value of rice, parents commonly use expressions such as "Rice is first," "Rice is the chief food of life," "We cannot live without rice," and "It is better to be without salt for one week than without rice for one day."[5] The most severe threat a parent can make to a child wasting rice is in the comment, "I will give you no more food!" It is rarely used, but seems very effective in disciplining a misbehaving child.

Parents warn children to accept and to offer food with only the right hand by use of the comment, "Why use the left hand?" This is supposed to be done to "teach the child to respect food."[6] Parents are vigorous in condemning a child who regularly takes his food and walks away from the others eating a meal. It is considered very bad manners for adults to walk about eating. Parents scold a child who insists on "roaming about" while eating by use of the comment, "Sit down and eat!" Wandering while eating is felt a sign of an ill-bred child because his parents were bad-mannered people. This value is expressed in the phrase "a descendant of that kind of person."

Children are taught to be aware of their thirst, and of proper ways to satisfy it. Drinks which do not quench thirst, such as tepid stream water, are believed less preferable than drinks of coconut milk, bamboo juices, juices from jungle creepers, fermented coconut milk and sap, and rice wine. When wet with perspiration from exertion, adults say they have "a fire inside" which is best quenched with a "good" drink. Rice wine is felt to be the most appropriate means of "replacing sweat" and to quench thirst. Children are allowed to drink any of the liquids used by adults to quench thirst if they have attained "reason." Before seven to eight years of age, rice wine is not generally available to children. At times of ritual feasting and especially at harvest, younger children may be given a small bamboo container of rice wine to drink. At parties mothers occasionally will quiet an infant with a sip of rice wine. Parents remind children often that rice wine is "food" and is to be treated with respect, and children are told to "show honor to the rice spirit." Children also learn that the juices of bamboo and jungle creepers can be used to prevent and cure a variety of illnesses, including diarrhea, arthritis, scabies, and all types of coughs. Children also are encouraged by parents to chew a betel nut preparation to avoid "a bad-tasting mouth and foul breath." Older children learn that "the mouth tastes warm and the saliva is loose" when they chew betel. Chewing often begins at five to seven years. Before that age children experiment with preparing betel but do not often chew because, as one four-year-old girl stated, "It is very bitter." Approximately one child in five over the ages of seven to eight years often chewed betel in Sensuron and Baginda.

---

[5] The comment "We cannot live without rice" is sometimes answered by a "sassy" Sensuron child with the comment *"àpàse pède leuan!* [The hill people are alive!]," which refers to the fact that hill peoples about the Tambunan plain often have such a short supply of dry rice that it is eaten only with guests and on feast days.

[6] The practice of treating the left hand as "unclean" is common among Moslem peoples. It may be that this Dusun trait is borrowed from Moslem beliefs. It is a common practice among "pagan" Dusun in isolated communities where the oldest informants "remember" the practice as supposedly common during the lives of their grandparents.

Children also occasionally smoke cigarettes made from locally grown tobacco wrapped in a variety of types of leaves. While adults smoke regularly, few children under 10 to 12 years make and use cigarettes. Sometimes a play group of 5 to 7 year-old boys will try smoking as an experiment. There are several narcoticlike leaves, tree barks, and nuts producing a feeling of lowered awareness to stimuli, or insensibility, and sleepiness when chewed, which adults sometimes use in place of a betel chew. Children are said not to be allowed to chew these substances unless they have "full reason," since these materials are supposed "to be the ones Dusun chewed before the betel palm was grown in the villages."

Dusun believe that anything edible must be washed to keep "dirt" from entering the body. Utensils are regularly washed in the belief that "dirt" can collect on these implements and find a way into the body. Children are instructed by parents to rinse the "dirt" from their hands before eating. The term "dirt" is a compound meaning active disease and disease-causing agents and is likened by Dusun to fecal matter. The belief is that "everything that looks dirty is dirty." Dirt in the food is believed to cause goiter, a condition in which foul matter is said to collect in the throat, making a large bulge. A person with goiter is said "to live like an animal in the jungle because they eat dirty food." Parents scold children failing to wash their hands or eating utensils with the expression, "You will get *gàak!*" At meal times most parents pay attention to whether their children have washed their hands and cleaned off their eating utensils before the meal. When a child begins to regu-

Ten-year-old girls playing in the Sensuron River while bathing.

larly wash his hands and eating implements before eating, he is complimented by parents with the comment, "There exists reason."

On completion of a meal, it is considered good manners to wash off the eating utensils and to rinse the mouth and hands. Eating utensils are often kept in a rack at the side of the house porch. It is a common sight after meals to see a Dusun family standing or squatting at the porch edge pouring water over eating implements, rinsing their hands, and loudly gargling and spitting water in clearing their mouths and throats of any "dirt."

Children are taught to bathe and groom themselves regularly in the belief that body dirt will get into food and cause goiter. As noted previously, children begin to take baths with their nurses, and by the time they are 7 to 8 years of age, bathe each day without prompting. Usually the clothes worn to the river also are rinsed off during the bath. Dusun adults rarely allow a day to pass without a bath. Children between 2 and 5 years old may be taken several times a day to the river and washed by their nurses to get them cleaned from mud and dirt acquired during play. Children of 7 to 12 years often spend an hour or more playing in the river while bathing. A form of tag is a common game at this time. Good personal hygiene is considered to be demonstrated by a child when he keeps himself as clean as possible; being clean is equated to avoiding the possibilities of dirt (sickness, magical harm) entering the body. Children receive little direct instruction in grooming their hair or in standards of being neat in terms of Dusun concepts of order. Between the ages of 7 and 12 they are expected to learn that people with "reason" are "clean," "neat," and "orderly."

However, a major technique of protecting children from illness during a crisis of an epidemic of disease such as typhoid or cholera is to allow them to become as dirty as possible. Parents believe that harmful supernaturals are much like themselves in not wanting to eat "dirty" food. Thus, they reason that a dirty child is safer from harm by a disease giver or souls of the dead than he would be if he were clean. Some parents believe this is the best way to protect a sickly child, and will encourage him to stay as dirty as possible without regard to the existence of an epidemic of disease in the community. The rationale for this action is expressed in this widely told folk tale, often repeated by adults to young children. This story was told by *sàndau* of Sensuron to his grandchildren:

> There was a man named *gàndud* who lived in the jungle with no family. While asleep one night two disease givers came to his house. One called "Are you there, *gàndud*? We can smell you!" He said "Yes." The second disease giver said, "We have come to eat you!" Then *gàndud* took all the dirt from the firepit and put it on himself. He called to the disease givers, "You cannot eat me for I am very dirty." Those devils came in and looked and said, "We must wash our food first." So they took him to the river. There he escaped while they washed their hands.

Some adults are considered by other Dusun to use this belief in dirt as a protection from sickness as an excuse for their laziness in not washing or grooming and in not making their children learn proper behavior.

Bowel and bladder training are supposed to be fully completed by the time a child is three years old. Incontinent children are harshly scolded by adults with a series of stylized expressions in the belief that an open display of lack of control of bowel-bladder is a form of direct aggression toward others. As noted earlier, Dusun children become aware very early of the attitudes of fear, disgust, and avoidance of adults concerning feces. They are expected by parents to know the potential harm associated with the "dirt" of one's feces getting into the bodies of others through food or from contamination of the eating utensils, personal effects, or houses. Children come to expect physical punishment if they defecate near the house. There are locations near a village where adults usually go to defecate. Children of five to seven years of age are expected to use such areas unless they are too ill to walk. Mothers will sometimes discipline a child failing to go to one of these locations to defecate by striking him with a stick on the back of the legs. A few families regularly urinate at the side of their houses rather than walking to the area for elimination. These people are considered "dirty" and "without reason" for such acts. It is not considered improper to urinate beside a house during a party. It is a grave offense of manners to defecate beside the house of a host offering food and drink.

AGGRESSION TRAINING

Parents are supposed to teach their children not to fight. Ideally a child is supposed to learn not to strike or touch another person in anger. However, adults feel that it is "natural" that young children fight one another. Most adults ignore fights between two- to four-year-olds so long as the event does not seriously disrupt adult business such as a court hearing or a ritual act. Parents will admonish a three- to four-year-old who tells another child, "I will get my knife [or spear] and kill you!" Fights between young children are a frequent occurrence in daily life.

By five years of age children begin to check their physical contact in fighting and to substitute "word fighting." Rather than hit out with fists or sticks, kick, or throw stones, children will stand close together and scream insults at one another. Usually, such insults are comments on some item of village gossip concerning the child's family, remarks about a child's lack of reason, his laziness, or his "dirty" ways. Sometimes children repeat some of the curses adults use in their quarrels and they may hurl feces or try to urinate on one another.

By seven years of age, children usually stop fighting that involves contact, except for occasional sharp outbursts of temper. At this time they generally substitute verbal aggression for physical contact. It is not uncommon for verbal aggression to be turned against parents. It is believed a very grave breach of custom for a child to strike a parent in anger, but it is not considered too serious a matter for a child to respond to parental discipline with insults. Parents usually respond to a child's verbal aggression with one of a series of stylized expressions: "You are like a dog, you are never ashamed of your acts!" or, "You have no ears to hear what I say to you!" Other adults know a parent is very angry with a child when these expressions are used. Such comments are made only when a child verbally aggresses against a parent, openly refuses to obey a command, or acts to destroy the property of other persons.

The malicious destruction of the property of another person by a child is considered by parents as an extremely serious matter, since such acts mark the child as a "rascal" and will cost parents fines and their own property in payment to restore damages to the property destroyed or harmed. Ideally Dusun parents are responsible for the acts of their children until they marry. Children known to be deliberately destroying property or stealing the property of others may be whipped hard with a length of rattan vine. Sometimes a bamboo stick may be used. Children ideally should be struck on the backs of the legs to keep them from "wandering into trouble," and on the hands "to keep from stealing." Usually a child hides before such events can take place. Before whipping children, or sometimes after a beating, a parent is supposed to say, "I am sorry for you, because I must hit you, but do not go and follow the other children the next time they destroy the things of other persons." Some children resist a whipping by cursing their parents while they are being struck with rattan or a stick. One ten-year-old Sensuron boy shouted at his father as he was being beaten, "Be careful! You are getting old for you are always angry all the time! I shall swear that I will not feed you when you get old and simple!" The boy's father responded to this "swearing" by saying, as he struck out with a length of rattan, "You would not be alive without your parents! You cannot swear at me, for it will not come true, because I made you—you cannot ever curse me!" As he finished this comment, the father spat vigorously while exclaiming *"pètue!"* to show his great anger. The boy twisted loose from his father and darted into the house, shutting and barring the door from the inside. Then he began to throw his parents' prized possessions out the windows, while crying and screaming more curses at his father. This behavior in a child is termed *mèguteal* and is the counterpart of an adult form of hysterical behavior termed *mèguhèd*. The diary notes which follow illustrate one sequence of *mèguteal* for a six-year-old boy:

Bright Sun: 80°F. TRW (Diary of Events) 13 May 63 Thurs. Bgda. p14

At 10:40 A.M. as I sat on porch of house 58 talking with *bèŋe* on color data I noted p. (male 6 years), son of d. in house 56, shoot a blowpipe dart at b.'s (his mother's sister) back as she sat on porch of house 57 talking with visitors from across the river. When the dart stuck in the cloth over b.'s shoulder, s. (p.'s grandmother) got up from house 57 porch, went into yard, picked up a 3-foot length of bamboo, went onto the porch of house 56, and struck p. sharply on the back of the legs with repeated blows. p. used the blowpipe as a spear and thrust it at s., who knocked the pipe aside and gave p. several sharp raps on the shoulders and at least one over the top of the head. p. burst out crying, threw the blowpipe down and rushed at s., beating at her with his doubled up fists. s. had said nothing all this time while p. was screaming over and over, "I will kill you! I will cut you!" s. turned away and went down the porch steps. p. followed, picked up a 2- to 3-foot length of wood about 2 inches in diameter and tried to hit s. on the head. s. grabbed him by the wrists and sat him down with a thump, then struck him sharply with the outside edge of her right palm on top of the head. p. fell backward to avoid more blows, then lay and screamed curses at s., rolled over, and began banging his

head on the ground until he cut his forehead on a stone. Then, with blood dripping into his eyes, he ran into house 56. I could see him through the open door as
he gathered clothing and small utensils into a pile. Then he began to carry these
items to the foot of the house steps, where he made a pile about 3 feet high and
about 5 feet across of women's and men's clothing, beads, fired clay cups, a mirror,
and eating utensils, two knives, and other household equipment. Then p. went into
the house and returned with a burning stick from the firepit and proceeded to set
the pile of goods on fire. All this while he screamed curses at s. and gave great
racking sobs. When the pile was well on fire, p. ran back into the house. s. came
running from inside of house 57 at the call of *bèŋe* concerning the firing of the
effects. As she stamped and shook out the flames, she shouted, "Only six years old
and you are mad already!" Inside the house p. was screaming and I could see him
beating his head against a house post and then turn and begin throwing gongs out
a side window, then a small (and very valuable) old jar, which broke as it hit the
ground near s. She shouted in anger, "You are mad!" and ran into the house. p.
dodged her grasp and ran out the door as s. struck him violently on the neck and
back with a water container and sent him sprawling down the house steps. p. picked
himself up and run to a nearby *ƙapoƙ* tree, climbed onto a high branch, and sat
there screaming more curses at s. She ignored him as she went about picking up
the partly burned and scattered effects. The group of 14 children who had been
watching the last part of this action gathered about the base of the *ƙapoƙ* tree and
began to taunt p. about being a "mad chicken up a tree."

10:58 A.M.—I went on talking to *bèŋe* about techniques of child punishment and
the concepts of *mèguhèd*.

The *mèguteal*-type behavior described here is not unusual for 5- to 12-year-old
male and female children. In two years in two villages we witnessed 20 (12
males, 8 females) incidents similar in form to this one, some even more violent,
and we observed and recorded by photograph and tape recording the behavior of
adults in eight *mèguhèd* incidents. Essentially *mèguhèd* actions are a limited form
of a culturally structured hysterical and violent behavior similar to that known as
amok (amoq) in Malay. Dusun adults usually destroy their own property, tear their
clothing, and injure themselves rather than attacking others, as is more common
during a seizure of *amok*. The acts of *mèguteal* are considered by Dusun as a child's
version of adult behavior during *mèguhèd*. Most instances of *mèguhèd* have a large
crowd of children watching from a safe distance. Parents treat *mèguteal* events in
children as the consequence of a child's being blocked or thwarted in his desires.

Dusun children also learn that they can deal with persons blocking their acts,
thwarting their desires, or trying to disadvantage them by two specific forms of
aggression, poison and magic. They learn from adults that sometimes arguments
can only be settled by use of one or both of these means. Children hear angry adults
shout, "Soon you will die from poison!" and learn that when a person uses this
expression he has committed himself publicly to killing his rival. Children learn to
fear this expression, as they note that individuals who have been threatened in this
way take great care in eating and drinking to avoid being poisoned. Children see

that every instance of sickness of a threatened person must involve a special divination to determine whether the illness is caused by poison or magic, and they learn that the female ritual specialist can cause the poison or magical harm to "return" to its "owner" and cause his death or harm. Children sit quietly as the ritual specialist chants the ritual verses while bending a special tree root into a triangular shape to represent a tree that has grown so the top branches return to the ground as roots:

> Look! This wood returns to its roots!
> So, the poison will return, stronger
> and more harmful!

Children hear adults regularly speculating whether the death of someone was caused by one or another argument with a person known to feel "strong" about being offended or disadvantaged in a dispute, in trading, or from having been cuckolded. Few adults die without their family and friends talking about the possibility of poison or magic as cause of death; most adults manage at some time in their lives to have a violent quarrel or dispute with someone in the community and many adults have bitter disputes with persons from other communities. If the deceased has said as he dies, "I am poisoned," his friends believe he was in fact poisoned. Children learn early that good hosts always sip or taste a drink before passing it to a guest to show it is not poisoned, and they learn to always touch a finger to any food and drink offered them and to lick it clean, or touch it to their tongue to demonstrate they do not fear being poisoned. Children regularly learn the magical forms used by adults to attempt to harm others. It is not unusual for a parent experiencing a sudden, sharp body pain to suspect that someone is trying to magically harm him. Usually, a discussion takes place between the adults of a family concerning the possible source of the harmful magic and the best means of returning or "sending back" the attack by "words"; an adult feeling afflicted by magic often uses this expression, "I am spoiled by clever words." The greatest fear of "clever words" is that a person will be made "mad" by such acts. Young children witness often parents secretly preparing and using magic to counter the harm they feel being caused them. The most common secret magic form used in Sensuron and Baginda involves stealing an object that "always touches the body" of the person to be harmed, such as a hat, skirt, or shirt, or securing a clipping of hair or a fingernail paring, and then saying one of a variety of more than 20 rituals for magical harm, such as:

> This I send to a——,
> I send these clever words
> to harm him.

There are also formal rituals said by the ritual specialists, which can be used in public to counter the aggression of other persons. These forms are done openly and are usually directed toward persons in other communities. Ritual magic involving personal objects of the individual to be harmed are usually secret acts done at night. Most often these forms are directed against a person within the community. As noted previously, a not uncommon act in personal aggression is to secretly smear feces onto the house posts of an opponent to bring him harm by sickness. The ritual and the secretive smearing of feces usually occur at the same time.

Children also learn that there are more than 50 curses which can cause magical harm when shouted at a person in the course of a dispute. These curses are often used in an argument resulting when one person seeks out and openly accuses another of attempting to poison or magically harm him. The accused person may respond to the open indictment by a counter-use of one or more curses:

1. You must die!
2. You will be eaten by a *rágun*!
3. Your entire family will die!
4. You will drown crossing the river!
5. You will choke to death!
6. You will die of a constricted bowel!

The concept of cursing is differentiated by Dusun from a threat to cause harm. A threat to kill another is viewed as a serious matter and can lead to a ritual fine, but it is not viewed as having a magical effect on the person threatened, as does a curse. Failure to respond to public accusation of using magic or poison can lead to sickness and death if the person accused is guilty of the act. It is believed that the most appropriate response to such charges is to curse the accuser.

Children are told directly by parents that no one should ever initiate use of magic, poison, or cursing since initiation of such acts will cause a person and his descendants to become cursed and doomed by the creators to ill fortune, sickness, and death. Children learn as well that the creators can also bring the punishment of *ausèŋ* (*seseàn*) to offenders violating traditional ways, especially as these involve initiating aggressive acts which harm others. Children also learn from observation that arguments between adults often are inherited from parents and grandparents and come to expect that these disputes may naturally continue for generations.

Children learn from parents and other adults that protection against attempts to harm by poison or "clever words" can be gained through carrying one of a set of ritually endowed objects to make the body "invincible." These devices are believed to provide strength to the owner and general protection against aggression by poison or magic. All acts of aggression directed toward a person are believed to derive from great anger and to be too important to the shaping and direction of life to simply be ignored, and trusting to luck that no harm will occur. Children are warned by parents that they cannot be like the "joker spirit," or *sumàsuai* (Williams 1965:18), who goes about leaving to its luck the events which affect it.

Most children of 10 to 12 years of age carry several small objects such as a piece of stone of a "strong" color (for example, "red with whiteness"), a bit of metal from an old knife of a female ritual specialist, or a dried nut from a rare jungle tree purported to give invincibility through the smell of its bark and the hardness of its wood. Sometimes these objects are only a piece of the cultivated marsh root left from infancy and carried as an indicator of the luck which had protected the child through illness and accidents of childhood. The other form of personal protection is most often in the form of a small container which holds water and animal fat oils which have been magically endowed by a female ritual specialist for use as an antidote against either a poison substance or "clever words." Materials for making such objects are ideally said by Dusun to be best when these are of "rare" and esoteric substances (heart of a wildcat, beard of a *ràgun,* toenails of a rhinoceros, and the like).

As part of learning the beliefs concerning aggression, Dusun children are warned by parents not to be quarrelsome, gossip, or say things in anger which might lead to "word fighting," and from word fighting to curses and threats to kill by poison or magic. Dusun have a complex scale of an ability to "feel offended" which is used to judge the seriousness of "speaking badly to or of another person." Words can make a person become "ashamed" (*eiḳomeḳum*), be "offended" (*ḳomous*), become temporarily "angry" (*àtàgèd*), permanently "angry" (*àrarègè*), or "hysterical" (*mèguhèd*). Most adults carry a mental score of the instances in which other persons have caused them to become offended, ashamed, temporarily angry, and such, and tend to make "word offenses" cumulative over a long period. Thus a man made ashamed several times by another person may in time become offended and perhaps angry on a permanent basis. The legal system of Dusun society recognizes the cumulative nature of such acts by imposing increasingly more severe penalties on an offender. Under traditional law an adult regularly speaking badly of others was not only considered as bad-tempered but was certain to be brought before a village council of senior males and heavily fined or even banished from the community. Parents tell children to avoid being quarrelsome since they believe the most certain way to become a victim of poisoning or magic is to give others a means to tally incidents shaming, offending, or angering them. Parents warn quarrelsome

Ten-year-old girls fighting with sticks. The girl on the left received a large scalp cut during the fight.

children with the expressions, "Do not become a habitually quarrelsome girl [boy]!" or, "Do not grow up to be a quarrelsome girl [boy]!"

Children are also given specific instructions not to lie or act in ways to cause other persons to become angry at each other through telling them lies or "making the fowls fight." Lying is believed to involve three persons, two friends and a third party trying to cause troubles between the friends. A very serious form of lying, termed "to spoil a name," which occurs when false accusations of stealing or cheating are made, is considered very close to the acts of magic and poisoning and is judged severely if proved before a village council. Parents regularly use stylized expressions to older children suspected of spoiling the names of others; they may say, "Do not lie!" or "You are a liar!" Younger children are often told by parents the story of a little boy who habitually lied to his parents:

> There was a boy without a loincloth. He used to run into the house and say things like, "I have seen a snake as big around as a rolled up rice harvest mat!" His parents would run out and look for the big snake. One day they did not, and the python snake ate that boy up because his parents did not believe his lies.

Parents also impart to children many attitudes concerning truth, justice, and friendship as they try to insure the child will not become a "bad" (aggressive) person. Children hear parents use the stylized compliment in praise of others as "a straight man" and discuss the worthy character attribute of actively seeking to set right unintentional harm or wrongs done to others. A child learns that a truthful person who restores a broken fence to keep animals from a rice field belonging to another individual is of worthy character. A child comes to understand that a person who voluntarily pays a fine for accidentally cutting down bamboo belonging to someone else when no one had seen the act is of worthy character. A child comes to know that the highest praise to be given in his society by one person to another is the expression, "This man gives justice to all."

Children are told by parents that justice to others involves devotion to truth as well as the unselfishness implied in the idea of worthy character. They learn the saying, "Justice is like a stone that rolls from the top of the hill crushing untruth on its way." Children understand that justice, like the stone, has no friends or relatives to sway its judgment and so goes straight to the heart of the issue (bottom of the hill) without regard for damages to liars. A Dusun parent will warn children not to be friendly with persons known to be untruthful and unjust, lest they become entangled in the other individual's fate. A Sensuron parent scolded an 8-year-old boy about a 12-year-old male friend in these terms, "Do not become a friend of this bad child; you will go to the land of the dead while alive!" The use of a curse implying burial alive is a feared event for most Dusun. Older children become very frightened when parents insert this curse into a comment made while disciplining them. Parents actively seek to impress upon children the value of "true friendship" with the Dusun folk saying, "A true friend is one who has a natural feeling of sympathy for you." Parents regularly tell their children that when one has only true friends, then justice and truth will exist and they need have no fear of poison or magic and will hear no "bad words" to make them offended, ashamed, or angry.

INDEPENDENCE TRAINING

Dusun parents believe a child should stop exhibiting dependent behavior by seven or eight years of age. They view clinging actions, complaints concerning cold and heat, food (for example, rice) on the face, wasting of food, tattling, lying, intentional destruction of property, theft, showing and complaining about fatigue, and regular complaints concerning the type and quality of food as signs of children's dependency. Parents are inclined to be very short-tempered with an eight- to ten-year-old who behaves in these ways.

Independence training begins at four and five years as children regularly hear and become aware that lazy adults who work badly "do the work of children"; they learn that when adults act in ways not generally approved in the community they are said to be "acting like a child." At about the same time that children begin to be aware that "being like a child" is an inferior state and not the most desirable condition of being, they are also made aware by parents that although children should not exhibit the signs of dependency, they are still to be limited in their choice and ways of acting. Children of five to seven years of age learn from their parents, by direct comment, that they are not supposed to roam about the village and participate in events suitable only for adults, that is, parties, drinking, and ritual feasts. Parents specifically warn a child not "to go astray" and turn into a "wandering" child. Adults feel that a wandering child is destined to become a "bad person," and wandering children are said to be the way they are because of a grandparent's behavior as a child.

When a child of five to seven years shows too much independence from his parents, he may have the label of "wanderer" publicly attached to him by parents in an attempt to try to control his displays of independent action. A child learns to fear the designation of "wanderer" enough that the public use of the term to him is usually enough to limit most extreme displays of independence. However, in Sensuron, at least two boys and one girl of five to eight years were causing their parents considerable concern with their "wandering" about the village; they regularly ate and slept in another house and often for several days at one time. They appeared to be unmanageable by their parents, even after several public whippings with rattan lines and bamboo sticks. The wandering girl was openly told by her mother and her mother's mother that "no one from the next house will marry you!" and that "anything asked, if it is not granted, she attacks her parents!"

A very dependent six- or seven-year-old child will be scolded by a parent with the expression "You are old enough not to cry!" whether they are crying or not; crying behavior is supposed a certain sign of dependency. However, parents may react to demands for or exhibits of independence by six- or seven-year-olds by comments indicating sorrow at the "loss" of a child, or anger because the child shows signs of perhaps being a wanderer. A few parents become offended with and ashamed of a child who is too independent, in an effort to control their behavior. The father of one of the "wandering" Sensuron boys refused to speak to the boy or to have him about the house for a period of three weeks while the father was offended; the father purposely turned his back to the boy whenever the child came near him during this time and commented that the boy was "stubborn" and "disobedient."

Parents do not make specific efforts to provide young children with special practice or prolonged exposure to cold, heat, pain, or fatigue. While parents do not insist on children's improving their knowledge or skill, since parents feel they have accomplished more than their children ever will, adults do seek to instill by direct comment to a child a specific regard and concern for personal property. In the evenings, fathers often tell stories about property to children as the family sits next to the firepit. This is done, as *ilos* of Baginda said, "so children will know the ways property is acquired and will want to add more for their children." In a father's stories about property acquisition, he details the precise classes and worth of property he has inherited and has earned since his inheritance. Such stories are often told as a continuing serial account, running on for weeks, with the father acting as a narrator and commentator in descriptions of his acquisition of valuable items of property (gongs, jars, land, and the like). In the course of such accounts fathers often tell children that they must seek to improve their wealth, since the amount he will leave "will not be enough to make all of you wealthy." It is considered bad manners and selfish for a father to refer to his property by saying "my property." Rather, it is believed proper that a father should say "property of my children" to instill a desire in them to be independent and to want to acquire more property to add to their inherited wealth. A "just" man and a man possessed of full reason is said to regularly encourage his children to be independent in acquisitions of wealth by referring to only his personal clothing, pipes, weapons, and such, which will be used as grave goods (Williams 1965:40), as "my property." These comments are viewed by Dusun as a proper way to train a child to aspire to success through social mobility in the community.

SEX TRAINING

Dusun adults believe the act of intercourse is arranged best by the fact of marriage. However, intercourse is considered also to have an element of chance associated with it. It is recognized that intercourse can occur outside of marriage. Drunkenness at a party is a typical "chance" occurrence of sexual behavior. Ideally, the social significance of sexual actions takes precedence over the actual consequences of such acts. Dusun adults really manifest great concern with the details of sexual anatomy and procedures of intercourse. This dimension of sexual activity is revealed clearly in the content of songs and folktales and in a broad, ribald humor freely used among and between the sexes and on special occasions across the boundaries of some social conventions related to sex.

The concern that sexual intercourse be kept in its proper social context leads easily to the impression that Dusun are personally anxious concerning sex activities. If the acts of individuals transcend the expected social bounds for sex activity, Dusun do respond with affect and with intensity of expression. Their responses and affect arise from a basic desire to keep a proper balance in fortune for themselves and their community by insuring that the powerful emotions involved in sexual behavior are expressed within the limits of social conventions. However, sexual matters and acts which are defined as possible and permissible are talked about openly with interest and attention, in a relaxed, tolerant fashion. There seems to be a quite sophisticated manner about sexual behavior on the part of Dusun adults, so long as proper social forms are followed.

Dusun children are not protected in the nuclear family household from learning either the details of sexual anatomy or of the act of intercourse. Younger children usually wear no clothing in and about the family dwelling. Older children and adolescents regularly change their clothes in the family dwelling without concern for privacy of any kind. Adults generally turn their backs to other persons when changing clothes. However, it is not unusual for a father or mother to walk across the house unclothed, in full view of young children.

Young children sleep near parents and have adequate regular opportunity to closely observe the acts of foreplay and intercourse. The springy bamboo house floor easily transmits the movement of adult intercourse. The fact of only a few feet of open distance separating a child and his parents during intercourse means children can learn also of the sounds of as well as the sights of intercourse. Parents make no special effort to shield children from the act of intercourse, except for usually waiting until all the children are quiet at night. There seems to be little concern by parents with whether quiet children actually are asleep, since intercourse at night, in the dark, is an act between married adults which is socially proper, expected, and justified by Dusun culture (see Chapter 3, the sections "Conception" and "Pregnancy").

Proper sexual behavior is believed by Dusun adults to be best learned by watching other persons engage in such acts in a "legal" situation. *sàdekàn* of Sensuron expressed the belief in this fashion, "Watch and learn from other people," in response to my direct question, "How do young children best learn about sex?"

Within the nuclear-family household young children rarely are censured for open sexual behavior. Self-masturbation, handling of the gentials, and exhibitionism are rarely attended to by adults. Adults look upon sexual play between children under four years of age with tolerance, in much the same manner as they view sex play in young animals. This tolerance has a limit at the point of oral contacts. Then the play is halted quickly, firmly, and without hesitation with such expressions of affect as "Are you animals in the jungle?" and, "Dogs have better sense than you!"

In the absence of adults from the household, sex play between younger children regularly occurs, but usually only as an aspect of other play. A momentary attention is given to some openly sexual activity and then play moves to other, nonsexual concerns.

Outside the family household younger children see and hear sexual behavior by their baby tenders and between older children and adolescents. It is not uncommon for a younger child to have his sexual anatomy examined and compared with other children's by a group of baby tenders.

In play about the house younger children sometimes discover older children in solitary or mutual sexual activities. If they keep a distance and do not tease the individuals involved, younger children can watch these activities. Adults will chase off both the child acting in a sexual manner and the younger children watching, often exclaiming, as one father did to his neighbor's children, "You are like monkeys in the trees staring at the stupid one there playing with himself!"

Intercourse between adolescents, particularly between a girl and a group of boys, sometimes has an audience of young children and their child nurses looking on from vantage points nearby; a favorite meeting place for teen-aged boys and girls in Sensuron was in an abandoned rice storage bin at the end of the village. Word of intercourse in this location was quickly passed on, and younger children would go to the area to peer through the openings in the bamboo side walls to watch the sex acts inside.

Older children are severely censured by parents if discovered in display of their sexual anatomy and acts of mutual sex play and intercourse. If parents happen to discover older children engaged in sexual play or having intercourse, they may take a bamboo stick to drive them apart. Nonrelated adults would scold the children involved, then ignore them. In the five instances of such behavior I witnessed in Sensuron where parents broke up sex acts or play by a beating, the expression *misàbu,* or "animal intercourse," was used each time as the older childred were scattered by an adult. This term is next to the lowest point on an emotional scale of Dusun terms for intercourse, which runs from the most positive term, *misàsàuà* ("to be married and have proper intercourse"), to the term *menesàsàuà* ("to have intercourse in animal-like circumstances"), through the term *misàbu* to the most negative term, *meut* (equivalent to an English four-letter word for intercourse). Parents having intercourse in their family house after their children are quiet are described as engaging in *misàsàuà* behavior. Adultery and sodomy are described by use of the term *menesàsàuà.* The term *meut* is used only in violent arguments between adults and as the most insulting term available to describe the sex behavior of another person's parents or spouse. Violations of the incest taboo within the nuclear family are described through use of this heavily charged term, since it not only denotes an illegal action but one which as well runs counter to the basic values of the society.

Adolescent boys often are instructed in the act of intercourse by joining in the activities of a group of boys engaging in sex play with one or two girls. Most adolescent girls do not become part of such groups, for the sanctions against such behavior are strong and can lead easily to a loss of reputation in the community. It does not really harm an adolescent boy's reputation to have engaged in group intercourse acts, but it does affect directly the prospects of a young girl for arranging a "good" and proper marriage.

Marriages are arranged by parents or representatives of the parents. A question of the girl's virginity usually arises when the boy's representative in the marriage arrangement reaches the point where discussion begins of the property exchange involved between the two sets of parents. A girl rumored or known to have been promiscuous has a difficult time finding a partner whose parents are willing to pay the full property price usually involved. If a girl objects to marrying a boy with a "bad reputation" for his sexual activities, she may be able to change the arrangements for marriage to delay or even cancel the agreements being made. A boy finds it difficult to reject a girl suspected by him to be promiscuous, especially when no one among the adults involved shares his conviction. However, if he generally expresses his concern about the marriage arrangement made for him, he can often delay the marriage for a time. Boys sometimes delay marriage hoping that the girl, whose features or behavior they find unattractive, will be caught in a sexual act and give him excuse not to marry.

There are times when older children, as well as adults, are able to engage in sex behavior with some impunity. At the times of celebrations after harvest, and at ritual and ceremonial activities, a great deal of rice wine is consumed. Then, there are many possibilities of intercourse and mutual sex play, particularly between older, nonrelated men and women and adolescent boys and girls. These chance meetings and acts, which usually occur in the dark away from the location of the party, are not viewed as harmful to personal reputations except when relatives are involved. Many adolescent girls have their first experience of intercourse at such times, when an older man lures her away from the noise and confusion of the party. Adolescent boys frequently have sexual contacts with older women at such times. The very rare instances of adult male homosexual contacts also are said by Dusun to take place at such times. Adolescent Dusun boys deny that homosexual contacts occur among them, other than occasional mutual masturbation.

As the Dusun children mature, they must learn a wide range of definitions of sexual surrogates. There are explicit definitions of who may touch other persons and where they may be touched, under particular circumstances (Williams 1966). They must learn which body parts can be exposed under particular circumstance and about ways to sit and stand and walk. These details are believed to be the child's responsibility for learning and knowing as he gains reason. Judgments by adults of a child's level of reason do not depend entirely upon, but are directly related to, the way children master the details of surrogates and symbols of sexual behavior.

RITUAL IN CHILDHOOD

Children regularly participate in ritual activities in two forms: (1) formal ritual acts conducted by specialists, and (2) informal ritual acts conducted for personal protection against sickness and ill fortune. As noted previously, children spend increasingly more and more time being a part of, or the subjects of, formal ritual. In the period from 4 to 12 years of age, children usually more than double the amount of time they participate in formal ritual activities. When a child is very sick, his parents usually ask a female ritual specialist to divine the nature of the illness and to effect a cure. In the years from 4 to 7, children are also brought into the adult world of ritual and conceptions of the supernatural by being allowed to witness ritual activities and listen to the verses of the specialists. It is during these years a child comes to know of the more than 180 different types of ritual acts in the eight major classes of ritual. As the child learns the names of different rituals, he also learns the very complex conceptions of the supernatural world held by adults. Children come to be aware that there are at least 70 spirit beings and some five forces, or powers, which can affect the lives of men. Children also begin to learn to group these beings and forces into the complex classes used by adults to distin-

Children watch as a kerabau dies from a spear thrust in its side during a ritual to prevent harm to rice seedlings.

guish between "good" and "harmful" supernatural beings and forces. By the time children are 10 to 12 years of age most can name the major supernatural beings and forces and describe their locations, habits, effects, or consequences. Some of the supernatural beings are used especially by adults to frighten children to sleep (see Chapter 4) and have been known to a child for as long as he can remember. Children are made especially afraid of harmful beings and forces and then reassured by adults concerning helpful beings and forces by folk tales told by adults which give details of creation and the creators and account for most natural phenomena (climate, matter, animals, plants, sound, reflections, time). These stories are often repeated at night when the family sits by the house firepit and regularly are told by aged grandparents on occasions of ritual feasting or formal ritual activities.

A folktale often told to children by their parents as a warning "to not do things which are forbidden and to not enjoy ways contrary to custom" is an account of the harmful spirit being called *kasub*:

kàsub causes people to laugh hard so they forget everything except enjoying themselves. They forget the difference between good and bad. When this happens, or people enjoy themselves too much, or hurt someone's feelings, *kàsub* appears. In the old days there was a big feast at a house, with lots of drinking, singing and the gongs being played. These people got a monkey and a dog to dance together and then laughed and laughed at the sight. The *kàsub* came and made the house sink under the earth, and all these people went with it except one man and woman who had not laughed and had said the dog and monkey dancing together was wrong, because it had never happened this way before. These two saw the *kàsub* there and told everyone. At nights near that place you can listen and hear the party still going on under the earth where the house sank into the ground.

By the time Dusun children reach 12 years of age they have been constantly exposed to and have usually learned the major outlines of a very complex and intricate system of formal ritual action and belief and are acutely aware of the links between these acts and beliefs and other parts of their social life.

Hearing stories about ritual and supernatural beings and being allowed to watch formal ritual acts with adults comes to full focus for the child when he becomes the subject of a divination or an attempt to cure illness. The forms of ritual used are adult forms. Children take part in and are subjected to adult ritual from the end of their first year onward.

Parents begin to specifically instruct children at about seven to eight years of age in ways to protect themselves from harm by supernatural beings and forces. Thus children learn to take ashes from the house firepit and sprinkle them in a circle around themselves while saying, "Do not enter my body! I sprinkle ashes into your eyes!" in the belief that this act will keep away souls of the dead. Children learn to repeat a number of personal ritual curses to drive away harmful beings. These are repeated over and over as evil (muddy) locations or places (burial grounds) are passed, or at night when out in the jungle or the edges of the village:

> Be cursed evil one!
> I have done nothing wrong!

or

> Look, I have no food
> with me to eat! Be cursed!

When children go out to play and are caught in a "bad day," they say a special personal ritual form of the curses:

> Hello relatives! Do not mistake me for an unfriendly person! We are all realtives to each other. So go your way!

As this verse is repeated aloud over and over, the child breaks off a blade of fresh grass or a leaf from a tree, places it over his right ear, or secures it in his hat or on his clothes, to show the harmful spirits a sign of kinship. Children are taught by parents that harmful spirits can be frightened away, confused, or misled by a number of specific actions. Children learn that most harmful supernaturals are afraid of fire and the ash products of a fire; when Sensuron adults go abroad at night, they carry torches of bamboo which are waved slowly about their heads as they walk to imitate a "fire being" in search of a harmful supernatural.

Many younger children continue to wear the ritually endowed objects and magical amulets of infancy, including the cultivated marsh root, to drive away harmful spirits, small applications of gum substances to make themselves sticky or to blind harmful spirits, bracelets and necklaces of seeds to make the wearer "invincible," and "sacred water" to make the wearer "slippery" to an "evil" spirit. As noted, at about 6 or 7 years of age many children begin to carry some form of magical objects as protection from sickness, poisoning, and magic. By 11 or 12 years of age, nearly all children carry or have easily accessible some form of magical objects. The ritual protections of infancy and early childhood are abandoned as "too babylike for adults," as one 10-year-old Baginda boy stated the matter.

Children learn to "greet the unfriendly ones" (for example, harmful spirits) with any one of a series of stylized acts and sayings. For instance, as a child comes from the house into the light of the rising sun, shining through the mists of the mountain morning, he is taught to "greet" the harmful spirits that "ride" on the sun's rays and in chill winds by nodding the chin upwards, spitting gently, and softly saying, "A greeting to the unfriendly ones from me!"

There are some informal ritual observances of a child's maturation. When the five- to seven-year-old begins to loose his first teeth, many parents note the occasion with the practice of "change the teeth," which involves taking an old tooth and placing it behind one of the longitudinal bamboo stringers on the house wall to insure that the child's new teeth "will be as strong as a wall." At about five or six years of age, many girls have their earlobes pierced by a sliver of bamboo to "make a girl beautiful." The piercing operation is usually conducted by the girl's mother, if she feels "brave," by placing the bamboo sliver against the outer ear lobe and then puncturing the flesh in a short, sharp thrust.

PHYSICAL PUNISHMENT IN CHILDHOOD

Dusun parents educate their children through use of a great variety of enculturation techniques. Many of these techniques have been described in the preceding pages. One of the most used and common ways of imparting information, beliefs, attitudes, and values on the part of parents is to inflict mild pain on a child by a number of types of physical punishments. These ways of physical punishment are not the only or the most important aspects of Dusun education. There are other events in enculturation which are of equal or greater importance (see Chapter 6). However, a brief description of techniques of physical punishment of children will provide for a more comprehensive account of the major features of Dusun enculturation. Some of the techniques described here have been discussed in the preceding pages and elsewhere (Williams 1965:87).

Few instances of a Dusan parent's use of physical punishment are as severe as the one described here:

29 April 1963, Monday, Baginda, 12:10–12:15 TRW

——— (female, 5 years) is crying loudly as she goes along the path to the spring, following her sister (female, 11 years). Her mother waits about 20 yards ahead, holding three water carriers on her shoulder. As the child comes up to her, the mother says, *"à-de-de-de!"* then spits loudly with the exclamation of *"pètue!"* The child screams at this and stamps her feet. The mother swings the water carriers (*tuŋas*) off her shoulder by the branch used as a support, and raps the child sharply on the right side of the head, knocking her over. The mother turns and goes on down the path, while the child lays in the mud beside the path screaming and throwing herself about from side to side. . . .

This particular act of physical punishment is beyond the culturally recognized definitions of appropriate use of pain as an educational device. Thus in Dusun terms the act of the mother can only be described as the consequence of her "anger" with the child and not as an expected form of punishment.

Dusun classify their regular use of physical punishment in enculturation in several distinct classes, comprising a number of acts involving physical contact between a parent and a child in an effort to "guide" behavior. The classes of punishment and the acts are:

1. To hit with a stick
2. To hit with a rattan switch
   a. To hit with a rattan on the back
   b. To hit with a rattan on the legs
   c. To hit with a rattan on the hand
3. To twist
   a. To twist a cheek
   b. To twist an ear
4. To snap with thumb and middle forefinger
   a. To snap a cheek
   b. To snap an ear
5. To slap with an open palm
   a. To slap on the cheek
   b. To slap on the buttocks

In two years of residence in Sensuron and Baginda more than 350 separate instances were directly observed of the use by adults of one of these forms of physical punishment. Analysis of the incidence or frequency of these classes of punishment provides evidence that demonstrates that parents rarely resort to the "hitting with a stick" or "hitting with a rattan" forms of punishment. More than 65 percent of all instances observed comprised use of "to twist" and "to snap" forms of punishment. Another 15 percent of all observations of physical punishment involved use of forms of "to slap." In the remaining instances of observation more than half comprised uses of forms of "to hit with a rattan." Only 8 percent of all observations were recorded of parents using the "to hit with a stick" form of physical punishment, and more than 95 percent of these instances involved punishments by parents. The remainder of use of the "to hit with a stick" form involved punishment by a parent-surrogate, usually a grandparent. In the uses of the "to twist" and "to snap" form of punishment the "twisting" or "snapping" of an ear was much more common than twisting or snapping of a cheek; about 60 percent, of the instances involved a parent snapping or twisting an ear to punish a child. Mothers administered most of the physical punishment meted out to children. Fathers tend to administer the punishment form of "to hit with a stick." In the instances of "to hit with a stick" noted, most involved a father taking a wood or bamboo stick to a child's legs or hands.

It is important to note that Dusun parents do not usually inflict great pain in most instances of use of physical punishment. The snapping or twisting of an ear or cheek, a slap on the buttocks or a flick on the legs, back, or hand with a length of rattan vine are not administered to hurt, disable, or cause long-term pain. The term "punishment" can give a misleading sense of description of the ways Dusun parents use their hands and objects to communicate certain information to their children. A more accurate way to impart the sense of Dusun physical punishment in education of children would be to use the phrase "corrective direction of behavior." Parents intend punishment to help a child realize the boundaries of acceptable behavior and to maintain discipline in the home and at vital work. The fact that a few Dusun parents occasionally become angry and really hurt a child should not be allowed to color the intent or the role of the physical punishment in Dusun enculturation. Again, that role must be viewed in the total context of Dusun education. Physical punishment is only one of a variety of techniques used in Dusun enculturation. As noted, physical punishment is not the most important or vital technique used by parents, but has equal importance with other patterns of behavior. It has been commented on here in some detail because it might be that a casual observer would tend to overemphasize and distort the place of Dusun physical punishment in child training, because of the many instances which can be noted if one lived in the center of village affairs for only a few days or weeks. The incidence of infectious diseases, the dangerous physical environment, the differences in child-nurse and adult-nurse care, the use of fright as an enculturation technique, and other events are just as vital, and perhaps even more crucial, to the development of a typical Dusun personality than is physical punishment.

6 / Patterns of enculturation

I HAVE DESCRIBED in the preceding chapters the principal culture traits and trait complexes which appear to me to comprise the culture patterns integral to the Dusun configuration of enculturation. In this chapter I will hypothesize the existence of ten separate patterns of Dusun enculturation. These patterns have been abstracted from the descriptive materials in the preceding chapters. Thus, the discussion of each pattern of enculturation arises from the observed facts of Dusun cultural behavior as reported in this text. Except for a chart giving some references to the location of traits and trait complexes in the description chapters, no attempt has been made here to formally account for and separately designate all of the many culture elements comprising each pattern. The purpose of this discussion is to summarize the details of the preceding chapters in a very brief, direct statement which can be used easily in making a general comparison between the process of Dusun enculturation and the enculturation processes of other societies. A list of "Recommended Readings" on the process of enculturation in 93 societies has been included at the end of this text. It is possible to compare patterns of Dusun enculturation with those in other societies through use of the suggested readings.

It is important to recall as you read that the patterns are abstracted constructs of relationships between particular events in Dusun enculturation. I have reviewed the data of Dusun enculturation and then proceeded to abstract those culture traits and trait complexes which appear to me to be closely related in their form, meaning, and function. I have labeled these groupings. The labels are taken primarily from the content of the pattern, but are also formulated with a concern that the "name" for the pattern be useful to other persons seeking to make comparative studies of data of enculturation, so terms are used that refer to similar phenomena in other societies. This chapter should be treated as a series of suggestions concerning the ways one can abstract and summarize the data of Dusun enculturation.

Pattern 1. The Nature of Children. Dusun children are not viewed by adults as possessed of innate worth or dignity. As children mature, they are supposed to grow into an ability to reason and so to protect themselves from supernatural and natural dangers. Full maturation of reason is not believed to occur before about seven or eight years of age. Before this age, because they are believed by adults to lack the capacity to reason and, therefore, an ability to act according to customary expectations, children are felt to be upsetting and bothersome to adults. Because of their lack of reason, children younger than seven or eight years of age are believed to be possessed of a natural self which is stubborn, demanding, disobedient, noisy, violent, quarrelsome, temperamental, wasteful, destructive of property, difficult to instruct, and quick to forget. Children of less than seven to eight years of age are believed to also be naturally inclined to illness, prone to accident, capable of theft, and without enough natural reason to be held responsible for major offenses under traditional law.

After 7 to 8 years of age children are believed by adults to be mature enough to be able to reason and so to develop enough character through learning to overcome their original nature. The period from 7 to about 12 years of age, when the reason of children is believed to come to full maturity, is felt by adults to be the best time to give children direct instruction in occupational and special skills and in teaching conceptions of "right" and "wrong" behavior. After approximately twelve years of age the natural self of a child is supposed to be mature and the child capable of independently learning the beliefs and ways he needs to know to behave as an adult.

Some children are believed not to develop reason, through some accident of illness, misfortune, or slowness of thought inherited usually from a grandparent of the same sex. These children are believed to become incurable wanderers and to become adults possessed of the natural self of very young children.

Ritual efforts are regularly made by parents to aid a child's reason to develop properly. A sickly child is assisted by parents to become well in order that his healthy body will lead to the conditions for further growth and increase of his reason.

Pattern 2. Birth as an Act of Alliance between the *teŋran*. The birth of a child, especially of the firstborn, is viewed by adults as a special social act. The act is believed to create a bond between the *teŋran* of the mother and the father, which is indissoluble by any other act on the part of the child, parents, or other adults. Even the death of the child is not held to break the alliance between the parent's *teŋran*. And divorce of the parents often has no real effect on the bond created by the act of birth. The special bond is believed made stronger by the birth of each child after the first one. The bond is made manifest, or tangible, by several social and ritual acts performed by each of the *teŋran* for the child. The special rituals said to promote the child's reason are performed on behalf of the father's *teŋran*. Reason is believed by the Dusun to be directly inherited from the father's *teŋran*. Rituals which promote health and strength for the child are performed on behalf of the mother's *teŋran*. A child's physical well-being is said to be directly inherited from his mother's *teŋran*.

When a child is slow to learn or sickly, his parents and their friends often assign the responsibility for these facts to one or the other of the parent's *teŋran* by identifying the obvious examples of slow learners in the father's *teŋran* and the clear instances of illness-prone adults in the mother's *teŋran* and then noting the child's resemblances to these kinsmen.

This alliance of *teŋran* is vital to a child as he matures in a community. In times of misfortune a child can call upon either his mother's or father's *teŋran* members for aid and support, and so through this pattern of enculturation every child born in "legitimate" circumstances has a very wide circle of relatives to assist him in his life. The fact of this alliance between *teŋran* means that the birth of a child causes a balance to be created in the social structure of a small Dusun community by providing a mutual focus of interest between social groups which might otherwise come into conflict in the course of fulfillment of their achievement of statuses of power and wealth.

Pattern 3. Rewards and Punishments for Behavior. Dusun parents attempt to shape behavior through use of a variety of techniques of rewarding children for behavior which is felt "good" and by use of particular types of punishment for acts which are said to be "bad." Rewards used by the Dusun parents make up the categories of (a) verbal rewards, (b) material rewards, (c) intrinsic situational rewards, and (d) action language rewards.

Dusun parents regularly use many culturally standardized speech forms to try to elicit desired behavior in children, or to approve and encourage repetition of desired behavior. Parents often use tangible remunerations in the form of special foods or gifts as incentives for repetition of approved behavior. Parents sometimes use the circumstances of particular social situations as a means of rewarding children. Thus the granting of permission for freedom of behavior at certain times of major rituals and other significant social events, such as birth, harvest, and so on, are rewards for a Dusun child. Children are also rewarded by parents through use of particular body movements which are stylized in certain postures, gestures, gaits, and facial expressions. There are many such action language rewards used by Dusun parents in their shaping of children's behavior. Children can easily ascertain approval or disapproval of their behavior by parents by the nonverbal messages conveyed in the way adults stand, walk, and use their body to gesture and their facial expressions to convey information.

In efforts to shape behavior to desired ends Dusun parents punish their children with the forms of (a) verbal punishments, (b) physical punishments, (c) intrinsic situational punishments, and (d) action language punishments. Verbal punishment includes use of speech sounds intended by the user to convey disapproval of behavior. Among the Dusun these uses are numerous and range from culturally stylized sentence-length utterances through single-word exclamations to a series of very stylized expletives used to convey disapproval of a child's behavior. Parents verbally punish children with threats of physical harm, threats of denial of continued nurture, threats of withdrawal of social privileges or of enforced social isolation, use of ridicule and shame, by use of statements calculated to induce fear and apprehension, and through use of verbal frustration, that is, by punishing children through a confusion of issues with volume of words or use of words with meanings unknown usually by children.

Parents also use blows and spatial isolation to punish children. Parents also send children away from the household to punish them, and parents may separate children in the living spaces of a household. Parents also regularly confront children with aspects of social situations which imply chastisement for being a child. Thus Dusun children learn early that they are not valued for their own worth, but for the contributions they make toward the parent's life ambitions and goals. This valuation of the child occurs implicitly in many social situations as the child grows up. Thus, the Dusun child is punished at times simply by being a child.

Dusun action language punishments include a wide range of threatening, menacing, abusive, and ominous gestures, body postures, and demeanors used by adults to give reference to their disapproval of a child's acts. Parents regularly impart their disapproval of children's acts by these means. A quite common action language punishment is for a parent to turn his back on a child while folding his arms across the chest with the palms tucked close to the body under each arm.

Pattern 4. Parenthood as a Prime Measure of Adult Status. Children are believed by adults to provide parents with a social position, or status. An adult with many children is felt to be a wise and responsible person. To be fully adult in a Dusun community an individual must be a parent. Each child born enhances the view of the community that the parents are mature and competent persons. A Dusun child learns very early that he lives in an adult world and is tolerated as part of that world for his value to adults in terms of adult concerns, plans, and activities. A Dusun child is tolerated and cared for by parents usually because he contributes to the adult scheme of things. Rather than being the Dusun "investment in the future," children are their parent's present demonstration of worth. This is not to say that Dusun adults do not "love" their children or have affection for them. Rather it is to say that children are "loved" by parents in ways which have to do with the relationships between the Dusun conceptions of the meaning of parenthood, adult status, and the raising of a family.

Pattern 5. Freedom from Work before Adolescence. Until about 11 or 12 years of age, most children are generally free from regular labor in the fields, hunting, gathering, and the tasks of making and repairing tools, houses, and storage buildings. There are few regular tasks in the household which occupy a child before about twelve years of age. Few children are regularly occupied in the care of domestic animals. The labor of cutting and carrying wood for the house fire, bringing water from the river for cooking, or preparing food is not often a regular part of a child's activities. Some children do work regularly at adult tasks. In many instances, these children are from families with an ill, absent, or dead parent. The older children, and especially those over the age of 10 years, may try to replace the labor lost to the family unit because of a missing parent. Generally in households with both parents healthy and present, children under 12 years old are not expected to and do not undertake regular work tasks. Some children do seek out regular work in the agricultural cycle or in the household, but most children do not do so and are not usually pushed into work by parents. This results in a long period of childhood which is generally free from continuous involvement in adult work concerns and activities, and so Dusun children are provided time, to about 12 years of age, to learn their culture at their own pace and style. Baby-tending activities do occupy much of the time of many children. This "work" is not viewed by adults as equivalent to labor in the fields or household chores. Children occupied as baby tenders are free to play and choose their routines. Hence, they rarely tend to see this assignment by adults as a "work" task.

Pattern 6. Concern with Supernaturally Caused Illness and Misfortune. Dusun parents manifest a continuing concern about the harm which may come to their children from evil and angry supernatural beings. From the time of pregnancy on through adolescence parents seek to provide children with protection from the illness and bad luck which they believe afflict a child not properly guarded through divination, magic, avoidance, purification, and complex ritual actions. Parents regularly worry about and plot to defeat the plans of evil supernaturals to hurt or affect the lives of their children. After about seven years of age, children are taught a series of ritual sayings and actions to try to ward off harm from supernaturals. These acts and beliefs provide children with a conception of sickness and misfortune and of proper ways to deal with such events, which condition and color many other aspects of their behavior. Children learn in this way the value of omens taken from animal sights and sounds, special objects, or from dreams which foretell the future.

Pattern 7. Supernatural Sanctions as Controls of Behavior. Dusun parents regularly use fear of the supernatural as a means of insuring that children conform to expected behavior. Parents tell children folktales with themes of violence which happened to a child because of some error in his behavior. Mothers sing to children with growth and health lullabies that contain threats of harm by supernaturals. Parents regularly seek to quiet children with expressions threatening them with supernaturally caused harm. Children are warned repeatedly that improper behavior can bring the wrath of some harmful being. The effect of such repeated threatening of injury, death, or worse, such as being eaten or buried alive, leads children to conceive of nature and the universe as being beyond human power to control or alter. In situations which are supposed to be controlled by supernatural beings and forces children learn to be submissive, quiet, and withdrawn.

Pattern 8. Differentials in Child Care. There are significant differences in the style of care given a child as he matures in Dusun society. In the first year of life a child is generally cared for by his mother. Any care given in this year by other adults is incidental and of quite limited duration. In the time from about two years to about five years of age Dusun children are cared for by "baby tenders." In this time the child is assigned to an older child, often the next oldest brother or sister in his family, to look after him while the mother goes about her daily work or cares for a newborn child while doing her work. Children may be tended in two different ways when looked after by an older brother or sister: they may be carried about and watched while the brother or sister plays with a group of younger baby tenders of three to six years of age; or they may be tended while the brother or sister plays with an older group of baby tenders, whose ages range from seven to ten years. In a younger group of baby tenders and their charges, the child is a part of a social group very much oriented to a young child's concerns and knowledge. In an older group of baby tenders and their charges a child is part of a social group whose orientation and knowledge is beginning to approximate those of adults.

Occasionally a two-year-old child will be tended by an adult, often a grandmother or sometimes an aunt. In this type of care the child is tended by the adults as they go about their daily activities, and so the child is a passive participant in social groups entirely oriented to adult ideas, values, and concerns.

There are instances when a child is not assigned to a baby tender; his mother continues or extends the care typical of the first year of life, because she has not become pregnant again or has no children or adult relatives to assist her in care of the baby. In this kind of care the two- to five-year-old child often undergoes an extended infancy due to the ways he is treated by his mother.

Between about five and twelve years of age children are no longer tended by older children or adults and become part of unsupervised neighborhood play groups, usually with a younger brother or sister in their charge for baby tending. As noted, if a 5- to 12-year-old child has the task of baby tending, he usually plays in groups with other baby tenders of the same general ages. A child of 5- to 12-years old not assigned the task of baby tending plays with other children of his age who also are free from the responsibility of baby tending. After about twelve years most children are free from baby-tending chores. So Dusun child care has several very different styles with a variety of opportunities for children to be exposed to and to experience quite different aspects of Dusun culture and society.

Pattern 9. Judgment of the Child as a Non-Person. In general, Dusun children are exempt from all responsibilities and liabilities of adults until they are judged to have enough reason to be held accountable for their actions. Children are not expected to behave as "little adults." Rather adults assume that children are not "people," that is, not adult beings, until they have sufficient reason to act like adults. Hence, a Dusun child is exempt from adult standards and expectations in his behavior. Children become aware early that it matters very little to adults if a child behaves as an adult. Adult comment, usually amused, is made noting that a child is behaving in some adult ways. Adults are amused because a child does not know that he is not capable of acting like an adult. However, a child is not encouraged to behave in adult ways. Most often a child is told he behaves as he does because it is natural for children, who are not really adults, to act in ways not expected or approved by adults. Children are treated by adults in many social situations according to the cultural judgment of the child as a non-person. This attitude is tempered by the fact that adults also believe children will finally mature into adults, given enough time and protection from supernatural harm to do so.

Pattern 10. Generational Alteration of Emotional Ties. Children learn early that they are allied with their grandparents, who act as their champions, protectors, and spokesmen with parents. Children soon find that their temperaments, faults, and attributes of character are supposed to have come directly to them from a grandparent of the same sex; faults or qualities of reason from their father's father or mother and faults or qualities of physical being from their mother's mother or father. A child becomes aware that he and his grandparents of the same sex make up special pairs of persons, which are cojoined across the generations by an emotional bond of a very durable nature. Grandparents of the child's same sex openly cultivate and promote emotional ties between themselves and grandchildren to insure that the child's ties to his particular *teŋran* are strong. When a Dusun child thinks of his *teŋran*, he tends to do so by the conditions and definitions set by his affective ties with the grandparents.

SUMMARY

I have presented a brief discussion of ten cultural patterns which I have hypothesized as comprising the configuration of Dusun enculturation. Each pattern has been derived directly from the data of enculturation contained in the preceding chapters. The purpose of the chapter is to draw together in some meaningful fashion the many details of Dusun enculturation so that comparisons may be made more easily between the data of Dusun enculturation and enculturation processes in other societies. I have made no attempt here to causally relate these patterns of enculturation to either specific forms of adult behavior or to patterns of adult personality. Such statements are possible at another level of abstraction. Such discussions would be premature considering the present state of knowledge of Dusun adult character and the limited discussion of many vital points in this brief text.

In order to make it possible for the reader to more easily relate the abstracted patterns of enculturation to the text, I have provided here page references for each of the ten patterns:

SUMMARY OF SOME REFERENCES TO CULTURAL ELEMENTS (ITEMS, TRAITS, TRAIT COMPLEXES) COMPRISING DUSUN PATTERNS OF ENCULTURATION

Enculturation Pattern	Pages in Text for Some Descriptive Details of Items, Traits, and Trait Complexes Comprising Particular Patterns of Enculturation
1. Nature of children	40; 41; 42; 45; 46; 53; 54; 58; 59; 60; 61; 62; 63; 64; 65; 67; 68; 69; 70; 75; 76; 86; 87; 88; 89; 93; 94; 99; 100; 101; 102; 104; 106; 110; 111; 118; 119
2. Birth as an act of alliance between the *teŋran*	45; 54; 55; 56; 57; 58; 76; 111; 112; 119
3. Rewards and punishments	61; 62; 63; 65; 66; 77; 78; 79; 90; 91; 93; 94; 95; 98; 99; 100; 101; 102; 103; 107; 108; 109; 112; 113; 119
4. Parenthood as a prime measure of adult status	34; 35; 39; 40; 43; 101; 113; 119
5. Freedom from work before adolescence	75; 76; 77; 80; 81; 82; 83; 84; 113; 119
6. Concern with supernaturally caused illness and misfortune	43; 44; 46; 47; 49; 54; 55; 56; 58; 60; 61; 63; 64; 65; 66; 67; 68; 69; 77; 88; 89; 91; 92; 93; 96; 97; 104; 105; 106; 107; 114; 119
7. Supernatural sanctions as controls of behavior	35; 36; 37; 38; 39; 40; 41; 42; 43; 44; 45; 48; 49; 57; 88; 89; 95; 96; 97; 98; 106; 107; 114; 119
8. Differentials in child care	40; 61; 62; 66; 70; 71; 72; 73; 74; 114; 115; 119
9. Judgment of the child as a non-person	70; 71; 72; 73; 74; 75; 76; 77; 100; 101; 115; 119
10. Generational alteration of emotional ties	73; 74; 76; 115; 119

7 / Changes in enculturation

I WILL DESCRIBE BRIEFLY in this final chapter the changes which have occurred in the patterns of Dusun enculturation because of events in Sabah and Southeast Asia in the recent past. The enculturation methods of small, isolated, and nonliterate societies contrast in a marked way with those used in contemporary Western societies.[1] Until recently Dusun enculturation was typical of small and isolated societies. Dusun children were trained in ways that made their enculturation a by-product of daily living. A firm and clear continuity existed between the facts and events of daily life and the enculturation experiences of children. The persons transmitting culture in Dusun society were primarily parents and close relatives. The personal interests of Dusun children made them active participants in the process rather than passive subjects in a formal setting. Dusun enculturation was aimed at teaching children to become knowledgeable and skilled enough to maintain and continue intact the culture of the society through the next generation.

RECENT CHANGES IN ENCULTURATION

With the advent of a new form of political control in September 1963, when North Borneo became the state of Sabah in the new nation of Malaysia, there were added changes in the nature of education in the country. The new Malaysian federal government increased the funds available for education to accelerate the pace of building new schools, training teachers, and bringing more native students into schools. However, the political disagreement between Indonesia and Malaysia from 1963 to 1966, which was centered along the borders between Indonesian Borneo and the Malaysian states of Sabah and Sarawak, caused delay and diversion of funds allocated for new and expanded educational efforts. A decision of the Malaysian government that Malay is to become the "official language" of government and schools led to a marked slowing of expansion of education by the mission and Chinese language schools; since English or Chinese has been used in these schools as the medium of instruction, and since there are very few Malay-speaking missionary or Chinese teachers available, these schools have not been expanded significantly since 1963.

---

[1] See Ralph Piddington, 1950, *An Introduction to Social Anthropology,* Edinburgh, Oliver and Boyd, pp. 179–188, for a discussion of the differences between enculturation in an isolated society and in modern Western society.

School textbooks now are being revised entirely in Malay, and the course of studies is being reoriented to Malayan culture, history, and literature.

These recent changes have altered the three-part educational system (see Chapter 1) which has been in operation in the country. Unless mission and Chinese schools can staff their classrooms with trained Malay-speaking teachers, their great influence and importance in providing most formal education in Sabah will sharply decline. It remains to be seen what effects these changes in the educational system will have on traditional Dusun enculturation patterns. There are now more than triple the number of Dusun students in secondary education than in 1960. However, still, in 1969, only about 15 percent of all Dusun children are in any type of school. With the settlement of the political dispute between Malaysia and Indonesia and a lessening of tension along the border of Sabah and Indonesian Borneo the Malaysian government may again turn its attention and funds to the improvement of local education in the state of Sabah. However, local political unrest continues as a serious government problem. When the language of the schools and government in Sabah become entirely Malay and the course of studies in school becomes oriented to Malay culture, it may be that yet another dimension will be added to change in traditional Dusun enculturation. A Philippine government claim to ownership of the territory of Sabah, which has recently caused a rupture of diplomatic relations between Malaysia and the Philippines, could divert funds and attention from the problems of education and also slow the change and development of schools in Sabah.

DIRECTIONS OF CHANGES IN PATTERNS OF ENCULTURATION

As noted previously, the three-part North Borneo school system has exposed a small portion of three Dusun generations of children to very different cultures and views of man. As the first two generations of children became adults, they changed some traits and trait complexes in the traditional patterns of enculturation to try to fit the ideas and ways learned in school to their own cultural system.

In Sensuron village in 1959–1960 there were 45 adults of the total population of 974 persons who had received some education in a mission or vernacular school.[2] No one of these adults had received more than five years of schooling. On the average these 40 men and 5 women had completed only the first two primary grades. Among the 11 village children who regularly attended the vernacular school, 8 were children of 3 of the adults with some school experience. On the basis of observations of and interviews with the group of persons with formal school experience it seems that those individuals appear to have introduced some changes into the traditional enculturation process. I will briefly describe these changes in Sensuron at the pattern level of abstraction.

In the pattern of adult conceptions of the nature of children, Western European

---

[2] In Baginda in 1962–1963 there were 32 adults of a total population of 751 persons with some mission or vernacular school experience. No one of these persons had more than five years of schooling. On the average these 27 men and 5 women had completed only the first two grades of primary education.

beliefs in the innate dignity and personal worth of each person have begun to replace the traditional Dusun valuation of children. The pattern of judging a child as a non-person has also begun to change under the impact of these same Western European beliefs about man. The pattern of considering parenthood as a prime measure of adult status has begun to change as schools make it possible for adolescents to achieve statuses with adult power and income before becoming parents. As children are occupied for longer periods of time in schools, the pattern of freedom from work before adolescence has also begun to change.

Too, the patterns of concern with supernaturally caused illness and misfortune and supernatural sanctions as controls for children's behavior have begun to change as Western European ideas of nature and technology, many of which are based on scientifically rational ideas, have made it obvious that basic conflicts exist between Dusun and Western explanations for many events.

There has been no significant change in the four enculturation patterns of birth as an act of alliance between the *teɲran,* rewards and punishments, differentials in child care, and generational alteration of emotional ties.

The rate of change in the six enculturation patterns which appear most affected by the school experiences of Sensuron adults varies from a moderate pace in the three patterns of concern with supernaturally caused illness and misfortune, supernatural sanctions as controls of child behavior, and parenthood as a prime measure of adult status, to a slower rate of change in the two patterns of the nature of children and judgments of the child as a non-person. The pattern of freedom from work before adolescence seems to have a very slow rate of change.

It is my feeling that the four patterns of enculturation which do not yet seem changed by experiences of Sensuron adults in schools are little affected because they are applied and used by Dusun parents well before school age, and because they probably are quite vital in maintaining the configuration of Dusun enculturation. It is often true in situations of culture contact and change that those patterns of a configuration viewed by the people of a society as basic to survival of their culture are the patterns less likely to be willingly changed.

It is my feeling also that the pace of change, in terms of the patterns of enculturation described here, is very much advanced in some areas of Sabah, particularly along the west coastal plain, where schools have been available the longest and where more Dusun children have been exposed to ideas of other cultures. Here, it seems that in many Dusun communities now linked by modern transport or communication with the state capital in Kota Kinabalu (Jesselton) all the patterns of enculturation are very much affected by changes introduced through schools. In this area it is possible now to find some Dusun families where the total configuration of enculturation has begun to change its form because of inclusion of a mixture of European, Chinese, and Malay patterns with traditional Dusun patterns. It seems clear that in another generation there will be Dusun individuals on the west coastal plain who will have been enculturated under a configuration of culture that will probably be very much changed from the one which has been traditionally Dusun.

The Dusun process of enculturation has worked well in the context of a small and isolated society. Children have been taught and generally have learned the beliefs and ways expected by their parents. Now the Dusun are one population in a state of a modern nation deeply enmeshed in the current affairs of Southeast Asia and the world. Dusun live now as individual citizens in a political entity which enfranchises them only when they are literate in Malay, English, or Chinese and are skilled in holding and acting in social statuses not usually part of Dusun culture. These facts are having profound effect on Dusun under 20 years of age.

The educational system of Sabah is contributing to a social situation in which many statuses which are earned, or *achieved,* are crowding out and overtaking statuses which are *ascribed,* that is, statuses into which persons are born. Some women are now qualifying for men's jobs in Sabah. Young men are rising to ranks of power and influence formerly held by old men. Persons from backgrounds of extreme poverty are rising to positions of modest wealth. Individuals find it possible to compete for achievement of statuses having merit and fame, although they are of very different social and cultural origins. A Dusun can now look forward to competing with Malays for senior government positions. A Dusun can now compete with Chinese for choice business locations, capital loans, and attractive government licenses. A Dusun can now aspire to be a teacher, or to gain a technical education to fit himself to be a physician, engineer, broadcast specialist, to edit a newspaper, write novels, or to be an artist. The growth in the numbers of statuses that Dusun and other native peoples of Sabah can achieve through education will promote even more rapid change in the country and so make social mobility even more possible.

However, this situation is not without its other effects. When achieved statuses begin to overtake ascribed statuses in a society, there usually is a loss of social cohesion in the group. Persons come to feel less a part of the society as an unrestricted individualism grows in status competitions. There is also a loss of communication between members of a society. Individuals training for and seeking special statuses, such as engineers, find it increasingly difficult to comprehend persons not educated to think in scientifically rational and empirical terms. This situation also produces conflicting loyalties. Individuals occupying achieved statuses often find they must choose between being loyal to another person because they are a close kinsman in need or being loyal to the institution they serve; a Dusun government official in charge of granting permits for lumbering a choice area of jungle may have to choose between the needs of a first cousin or the good of the society as a whole. Also, there is a general reduction of obligatory norms, that is, a diminuation of good manners. Persons become less concerned with maintaining an appearance of manners and ethics with others in competition for achieved statuses. There often is an increase in social aggression in a society in which achieved statuses overtake ascribed statuses.

THE FUTURE

It is clear to me that the traditional Dusun enculturation process will change profoundly in the years ahead. I have no way of knowing whether the changes in this one configuration of Dusun culture will be "good" or "bad" in terms of what is reasonable and correct for Dusun. I would prefer to allow the Dusun, in the context of their larger society, to make their own judgments of worth concerning cultural changes. It is much too easy for ethnographers to become afflicted with a bad case of "primitive rose-budism," that is, to want to protect and maintain a traditional culture which is seen as having unique merit.

I believe the Dusun must become aware of their own cultural heritage and then decide themselves how to best retain those aspects of that "old" culture which will benefit all. They must learn how to select those new ways which can assist everyone in the society to lead lives which by Dusun standards and within the context of Dusun cultural values are productive and meaningful.

I cannot select those culture traits and trait complexes, patterns, or configurations of Dusun culture which will best promote the future interests of the Dusun. I understand, appreciate, and am sympathetic to Dusun concerns. I believe I have even learned to "think" about some things in a Dusun manner. However, my personal destiny is inextricably wound into the fate of my own society and culture. It would be ethically questionable and a great disservice to the Dusun were I to decide how Dusun ought to live their lives, raise their children, and plan for their future. It is, I believe, a very subtle form of tyranny to try to plan the destinies of other cultures. Planned cultural change is a valuable device for maintaining order and cohesion in a society. However, change must be planned and directed by members of the culture and not imposed from without, or directed by external uses of power, applied in a culture-bound and unthinking manner.

I hope for the best for my Dusun friends as they inevitably move into the mainstream of our complex and often difficult modern world. I hope to have the opportunity to conduct more research on the process of enculturation that will evolve in Dusun life. If I do not, then this record possibly will allow others to do so and to continue the effort to describe the way Dusun children learn the culture of their variety of human society.

References cited

ABERLE, D., 1951, "The Psychosocial Analysis of a Hopi Life History," *Comparative Psychology Monographs* 21:1–133.

ALLPORT, G., 1942, *The Use of Personal Documents in Psychological Science,* Bulletin No. 49. New York: Social Science Research Council.

ANTONISSEN, A., 1958, *Kadazan-English and English-Kadazan Dictionary.* Canberra: Government Printing Office.

BARNOUW, V., 1949, "The Phantasy World of a Chippewa Woman," *Psychiatry* 12:67–76.

———, 1963, *Culture and Personality.* Homewood, Ill.: The Dorsey Press.

BARRY, H., III., 1957, "Relationships between Child Training and the Pictorial Arts," *Journal of Abnormal and Social Psychology* 54:380–383.

———, M. K. BACON, and I. L. CHILD, 1957, "A Cross-Cultural Survey of Some Sex Differences in Socialization," *Journal of Abnormal and Social Psychology* 55:327–332.

———, I. L. CHILD, and M. K. BACON, 1959, "Relation of Child Training to Subsistence Economy," *American Anthropologist* 61:51–63.

BARKER, R. G. and L. S. BARKER, 1961, "Behavior Units for the Comparative Study of Cultures," in *Studying Personality Cross-Culturally,* B. Kaplan, ed. New York: Harper & Row, pp. 457–476.

——— and H. F. WRIGHT, 1951, *One Boy's Day. A Specific Record of Behavior.* New York: Harper & Row.

———, 1955, *The Midwest and its Children, The Psychological Ecology of an American Town.* New York: Harper & Row.

BATESON, G. and M. MEAD, 1942, *Balinese Character: A Photographic Analysis.* New York: New York Academy of Sciences, Special Publication No. 2.

BEATTIE, J., 1965, *Understanding an African Kingdom: Bunyoro.* New York: Holt, Rinehart and Winston, Inc.

BLUMER, H., 1939, "An Appraisal of Thomas and Znaniecki's *The Polish Peasant in Europe and America,*" *Critique of Research in the Social Sciences,* No. 1, New York: Social Science Research Council.

CENSE, A. A., and E. M. UHLENBECK, 1958, "Critical Survey of Studies on the Languages of Borneo." The Hague: Koninklijk Instituut vor Taal-, Land-en Volkenkunde, Bibliographical Series 2.

COBBOLD COMMISSION, 1962 (June 21), *Report of the Commission of Enquiry, North Borneo and Sarawak, 1962.* Kuching: Government Printing Office.

COHEN, Y. A., 1961, *Social Structure and Personality.* New York: Holt, Rinehart and Winston, Inc.

———, 1964, *The Transition from Childhood to Adolescence.* Chicago: Aldine.

COON, C. S., 1965, *The Living Races of Man.* New York: Knopf.

COTTER, C., W. G. SOLHEIM, II, and T. R. WILLIAMS, 1962, *North Borneo, Brunei and Sarawak: A Bibliography of Historical, Administrative and Ethnographic Sources.* Hilo, Hawaii: Peace Corps Training Project for North Borneo and Sarawak, July 1962.

——— and S. Saito, 1965, *Bibliography of English Language Sources on Human Ecology: Eastern Malaysia and Brunei.* 2 vols. Honolulu: Department of Asian Studies, University of Hawaii (see Cotter, Solheim, and Williams 1962).

Dennis, W., 1940, *The Hopi Child.* New York: Appleton.

Dollard, J., 1935, *Criteria for the Life History.* New York: P. Smith.

DuBois, C., 1944, *The People of Alor.* Minneapolis: University of Minnesota Press.

Dyen, I., 1965, *Lexicostatistical Classification of the Austronesian Languages.* Baltimore: Waverly Press.

Eggan, D., 1949, "The Significance of Dreams for Anthropological Research," *American Anthropologist* 51:177–198.

———, 1952, "The Manifest Content of Dreams: A Challenge to Social Science," *American Anthropologist* 54:469–485.

Ethnology: An International Journal of Cultural and Social Anthropology.

Evans, I. H. N., 1913, "Folk Stories of the Tempasuk and Tuaran Districts, British North Borneo," *The Journal of the Royal Anthropological Institute of Great Britain and Ireland* 43:422–479.

———, 1922, *Among Primitive Peoples in Borneo.* London: Seeley, Service and Company.

———, 1923, *Studies in Religion, Folklore and Custom in British North Borneo and the Malaya Peninsula.* Cambridge: Cambridge.

———, 1949, "Dusun Customary Law at Kadamaian," *Journal of the Malayan Branch of the Royal Asiatic Society* 22:31–37.

———, 1950, "Some Dusun Measures and the Classification of Domestic Animals," *Sarawak Museum Journal* 5:193–195.

———, 1951, "Fifty Dusun Riddles," *Sarawak Museum Journal* 5:553ff.

———, 1952, "Notes on the Bajaus and Other Coastal Tribes of North Borneo," *Journal of the Malayan Branch of the Royal Asiatic Society* 25:48–55.

———, 1953, *The Religion of the Tempasuk Dusun of North Borneo.* New York: Cambridge.

———, 1954, "More Dusun Riddles," *Sarawak Museum Journal* 6:20–35.

———, 1955a, "Visits to the Banggi Island and Rungus Dusuns," *Sarawak Museum Journal* 6:218–232.

———, 1955b, "Some Dusun Proverbs and Proverbial Sayings," *Sarawak Museum Journal* 6:233–244.

———, 1955c, "Some Dusun Fables," *Sarawak Museum Journal,* 6:245–247.

———, 1955d, "Kadamaian Dusun Headmen of Former Times," *Sarawak Museum Journal* 6:248–249.

———, 1955e, "Stories from North Borneo," *Sarawak Museum Journal* 6:250–253.

———, 1956, "Return to Tambutuon," *Sarawak Museum Journal* 7:131–152.

Fischer, J. and A. Fischer, 1966, *The New Englanders of Orchard Town, U.S.A.,* in Six Cultures Series, Vol. 5, B. Whiting, ed. New York: Wiley.

Freeman, J. D., 1955, *Iban Agriculture.* Colonial Research Study, No. 18. London: Her Majesty's Stationery Office.

Geddes, W. R., 1954, *The Land Dayaks of Sarawak.* Colonial Research Study, No. 14. London: Her Majesty's Stationery Office.

———, 1961, *Nine Dayak Nights.* New York: Oxford.

Glynn-Jones, M., 1953, *The Dusun of the Penampang Plains in North Borneo,* Foreign Office Publication DB 75017/1/2214/80/3155. London: Foreign Office.

Goodman, M. E., 1967, *The Individual and Culture.* Homewood, Ill.: The Dorsey Press.

Gossens, A. L., 1924, "A Grammar and Vocabulary of the Dusun Language," *Journal of the Malayan Branch of the Royal Asiatic Society* 2:87–220.

Hallowell, A. I., 1947, "Myth, Culture and Personality," *American Anthropologist* 49: 544–556.

Haring, D. G., 1956, *Personal Character and Cultural Milieu.* Syracuse: Syracuse University Press.

Hart, Don V., Phya Anuman Rajadhon, and Richard J. Coughlin, 1965, *Southeast*

Asian Birth Customs: Three Studies in Human Reproduction. New Haven: Human Relations Area Files.

HEINICKE, C. and B. B. WHITING, 1953, *Bibliography on Personality and Social Development of the Child and Selected Ethnographic Sources on Child Training,* Pamphlet No. 10. New York: Social Science Research Council.

HENRY, J., 1958, "The Personal Community and Its Invariant Properties," *American Anthropologist* 60:827–831.

——, 1960, "A Cross-Cultural Outline of Education," *Current Anthropology* 1:267–305.

——, and Z. HENRY, 1944, *Doll Play of Pilagá Indian Children,* Research Monograph No. 4. New York: American Orthopsychiatric Association.

HEYER, V., 1953, "Relations between Men and Women in Chinese Stories," in *The Study of Culture at a Distance,* M. Mead and R. Metraux, eds., Chicago: University of Chicago Press, pp. 221–234.

HEYNS, R. W. and R. LIPPITT, 1954, "Systematic Observational Techniques," in *Handbook of Social Psychology,* Vol. 1, G. Lindzey, ed., Cambridge, Mass.: Addison-Wesley, pp. 370–404.

HILGER, SISTER I., 1960, *Field Guide to the Ethnological Study of Child Life.* New Haven, Conn.: Human Relations Area Files.

HOLLEY, S., 1955, "The Origins of the Idahan People," *Sarawak Museum Journal* 6:257–262.

HONIGMANN, J., 1954, *Culture and Personality.* New York: Harper & Row.

——, 1967, *Personality in Culture.* New York: Harper & Row.

HSU, F. L. K., 1953, *Americans and Chinese: Two Ways of Life.* New York: Abelard-Schuman, Ltd.

——, ed., 1954, *Aspects of Culture and Personality: A Symposium.* New York: Abelard-Schuman, Ltd.

——, ed., 1961, *Psychological Anthropology.* Homewood, Ill.: The Dorsey Press.

HULSE, F. S., 1963, *The Human Species.* New York: Random House, Inc.

JENSEN, E., 1965, "Hill Rice; An Introduction to the Hill Padi Cult of the Sarawak Iban," *Folk: Dansk Etnografisk Tidsskrift* 7:43–88.

——, 1966, "Iban Birth," *Folk: Dansk Etnografisk Tidsskrift* 8:165–178.

JONES, L. W., 1962, *North Borneo, Report on the Census of Population Taken 10th August, 1960.* Kuching: Government Printing Office.

KAPLAN, B., ed., 1961, *Studying Personality Cross-Culturally.* New York: Harper & Row.

KLUCKHOHN, C., 1954, "Culture and Behavior," in *Handbook of Social Psychology,* Vol. 2, G. Lindzey, ed., Cambridge, Mass.: Addison-Wesley, pp. 921–976.

——, H. A. MURRAY, and D. SCHNEIDER, 1953, *Personality in Nature, Society and Culture,* 2d ed. New York: Knopf.

KROEBER, A. L., 1948, *Anthropology.* New York: Harcourt.

LANDY, D., 1960, "Methodological Problems of Free Doll Play as an Ethnographic Field Technique," in *Men and Cultures,* A. F. C. Wallace, ed. Philadelphia: University of Pennsylvania Press, pp. 162–163.

LANTIS, M., 1953, "Nunivak Eskimo Personality as Revealed in the Mythology," *Anthropological Papers of the University of Alaska* 2:109–174.

LEACH, E. R., 1950, "Social Science Research in Sarawak," *Colonial Research Studies,* No. 1. London: Her Majesty's Stationery Office.

LEIGHTON, A. and D. LEIGHTON, 1949, *Gregorio, the Hand Trembler,* Peabody Museum Papers, Vol. 40. Cambridge, Mass.: Harvard University Press.

LEVINE, R. and B. LEVINE, 1966, *Nyansongo: A Gusii Community in Kenya,* in Six Cultures Series, Vol. 2, B. Whiting, ed. New York: Wiley.

LEWIS, O., 1959, *Five Families: Mexican Case Studies in the Culture of Poverty.* New York: Basic Books.

——, 1961, *The Children of Sanchez: Autobiography of a Mexican Family.* New York: Random House, Inc.

——, 1966, *La Vida.* New York: Random House, Inc.

LIE-INJO LUAN ENG, J. CHIN and T. S. TI, 1969, "Glucose 6 phosphate dehydrogenase deficiency in Brunei, Sabah and Sarawak," *Annals of Human Genetics* 28:173–176.

LIVINGSTONE, FRANK B., 1967, *Abnormal Hemoglobins in Human Populations*. Chicago: Aldine.

LORENZ, K., 1952, *King Solomon's Ring: New Light on Animal Ways*, Majorie K. Wilson, tr., New York: Thomas Y. Crowell.

LUERING, H. L. E., 1897, "A Vocabulary of the Dusun Dialect," *Journal of the Straits Branch of the Royal Asiatic Society*, pp. 1–29.

MARETZKI, T. and H. MARETZKI, 1966, *Taira: An Okinawan Village*, in Six Cultures Series, Vol. 7, B. Whiting, ed. New York: Wiley.

MEAD, M., 1928a, *Coming of Age in Samoa*. New York: Morrow.

——, 1928b, "The Role of the Individual in Samoan Culture," *Journal of the Royal Anthropological Institute of Great Britain and Ireland* 58:481–495.

——, 1930a, "Adolescence in Primitive and Modern Society," in *The New Generation*, V. F. Calverton and S. D. Schmalhausen, ed. New York: Citadel.

——, 1930b, *Growing up in New Guinea*. New York: Morrow.

——, 1931, "The Primitive Child," in *A Handbook of Child Psychology*, C. Murchison, ed. Worcester, Mass.: Clark University Press, pp. 669–687.

——, 1932, "An Investigation of the Thought of Primitive Children, with Special Reference to Animism," *Journal of the Royal Anthropological Institute of Great Britain and Ireland* 62:173–190.

——, 1937, *Cooperation and Competition among Primitive Peoples*. New York: McGraw-Hill.

——, 1939–1940, "The Concept of Plot in Culture," *Transactions of the New York Academy of Sciences* 2:24–31.

——, 1940, "Social Change and Cultural Surrogates," *Journal of Educational Sociology* 14:92–104.

——, 1946, "Research on Primitive Children," in *Manual of Child Psychology*, L. Charmichael, ed. New York: Wiley, pp. 735–780.

——, 1947, "Age Patterning in Personality Development," *American Journal of Orthopsychiatry* 17:231–240.

——, 1949, *Male and Female: A Study of the Sexes in a Changing World*. New York: Morrow.

——, 1952, "Some Relationships between Social Anthropology and Psychiatry," in *Dynamic Psychiatry*, F. Alexander and H. Ross, eds. Chicago: University of Chicago Press, pp. 401–488.

——, 1953, "National Character," in *Anthropology Today*, A. L. Kroeber, ed. Chicago: University of Chicago Press, pp. 642–667.

——, 1954a, "Some Theoretical Considerations on the Problem of Mother-Child Separation," *American Journal of Orthopsychiatry* 24:471–483.

——, 1954b, "The Swaddling Hypothesis: Its Reception," *American Anthropologist* 56: 395–409.

——, 1956, *New Lives for Old: Cultural Transformations—1928–1953*. New York: Morrow.

——, 1963a, "Socialization and Enculturation," *Current Anthropology* 4:184–188.

——, 1963b, "Anthropology and an Education for the Future," in *The Teaching of Anthropology*, D. Mandelbaum, G. W. Lasker, and E. M. Albert, eds. Washington, D. C.: American Anthropological Association, Memoir 94:595–607.

——, and F. C. MACGREGOR, 1951, *Growth and Culture: A Photographic Study of Balinese Childhood*. New York: Putnam.

MINTURN, L. and J. HITCHCOCK, 1966, *The Rājpūts of Khalapur, India*, in Six Cultures Series, Vol. 3, B. Whiting, ed. New York: Wiley.

——, and W. W. LAMBERT, 1964, *Mothers of Six Cultures: Antecedents of Child Rearing*. New York: Wiley.

MORRIS, H. S., 1966, "Review of T. R. Williams, The Dusun: A North Borneo Society," *Man: The Journal of the Royal Anthropological Institute* (n.s.) 1:426.

MURDOCK, G. P., 1954, *Outline of World Cultures*. New Haven, Conn.: Human Relations Area Files.

——, 1967, *Ethnographic Atlas*. Pittsburgh: University of Pittsburgh Press.

——, C. S. FORD, A. E. HUDSON, R. KENNEDY, L. W. SIMMONS, and J. W. M. WHITING, 1961, *Outline of Cultural Materials*, 4th rev. ed. New Haven, Conn.: Human Relations Area Files.

NYDEGGER, W. and C. NYDEGGER, 1966, *Tarong: An Ilocos Barrio in the Philippines*, in Six Cultures Series, Vol. 6, B. Whiting, ed. New York: Wiley.

PIAGET, J., 1955, *The Construction of Reality in the Child*. London: Routledge.

POWDERMAKER, H., 1966, *Stranger and Friend: The Way of an Anthropologist*. New York: Norton.

RITCHIE, J., 1957, *Childhood in Rakau, the First Five Years of Life*, Victoria University Publications in Psychology, No. 10. Wellington: Victoria University, Department of Psychology.

ROHEIM, G., 1941, "Play Analysis with Normanby Island Children," *American Journal of Orthopsychiatry* 11:524–549.

ROMNEY, K. and R. ROMNEY, 1966, *The Mixtecans of Juxtlahuaca, Mexico*, in Six Cultures Series, Vol. 4, B. Whiting, ed. New York: Wiley.

RUTTER, O., 1922, *British North Borneo*. London: Constable.

——, 1929, *The Pagans of North Borneo*. London: Hutchinson.

SARGENT, S. S. and M. W. SMITH, eds., 1949, *Culture and Personality*, Proceedings of an Inter-Disciplinary Conference under the Auspices of the Viking Fund, November, 1947. New York: Viking Fund Publications in Anthropology.

SEARS, R. R., E. E. MACCOBY, and H. LEVIN, 1957, *Patterns of Child Rearing*. New York: Harper & Row.

SPIRO, M., 1958, *Children of the Kibbutz*. Cambridge, Mass.: Harvard University Press.

SPITZ, R., 1946, "Anaclitic Depression," *Psychoanalytic Study of the Child* 2:313–342.

STAAL, J., 1923–1925, "The Dusuns of North Borneo," *Anthropos* 18–19:958–977; 20:120–138:929–951.

——, 1926, "The Dusun Language," *Anthropos* 21:938–951.

VELLA, F. and D. TAVARIA, 1961, "Haemoglobin variants in Sarawak and North Borneo," *Nature* 190:729–730.

VON SENDEN, M., 1932, *Space and Sight; The Perception of Space and Shape in the Congenitally Blind Before and After Operation*, Peter Health, tr., New York: Free Press.

WALLACE, A. F. C., 1950, "A Possible Technique for Recognizing Psychological Characteristics of the Ancient Maya from Analysis of Their Art," *American Imago* 7:245.

——, 1961, *Culture and Personality*. New York: Random House Inc.

WEINBERG, S. K., 1958, *Culture and Personality; A Study of Four Approaches*. Washington, D. C.: Public Affairs Press.

WHITE, E., 1955a, "A Dusun Fertility Rite," *Sarawak Museum Journal* 6:254–256.

——, 1955b, "Two Dusun Jars," *Sarawak Museum Journal* 6:307–309.

——, 1959, "Dusun Bamboo Fertility Rites," *Sarawak Museum Journal* 9:118–120.

WHITING, B. B. 1963, *Six Cultures*. New York: Wiley.

——, and C. HEINICKE, 1953, *Selected Ethnographic Sources on Child Training and Bibliography on Personality and Social Development of the Child*, Pamphlet No. 10. New York: Social Science Research Council.

WHITING, J. W. M. and I. L. CHILD, 1953, *Child Training and Personality: A Cross-Cultural Study*. New Haven, Conn.: Yale University Press.

——, I. L. CHILD, W. W. LAMBERT, and others, 1966, *Field Guide for a Study of Socialization*, Vol. 1, New York: Wiley (also privately circulated in mimeograph form, 1954, as "Field Guide for the Study of Socialization in Five Societies").

——, R. KLUCKHOHN, and A. ANTHONY, 1958, "The Function of Male Initiation Ceremonies at Puberty," in *Readings in Social Psychology*, E. E. Maccoby, T. M. Newcomb, and E. L. Hartley, eds. New York: Holt, Rinehart and Winston, Inc.

——, and T. K. LANDAUER, 1964, "Infantile Stimulation and Adult Stature of Human Males," *American Anthropologist* 66:1007–1018.

WILKINSON, R. J., 1943, *A Malay-English Dictionary (Romanised)*. Tokyo: Daitāa Syuppan Kabusiki Kaisya.

WINSTEDT, R. O., 1958, *An Unabridged English-Malay Dictionary.* Singapore: Marican and Sons.

WILLIAMS, T. R., 1958, "The Structure of the Socialization Process in Papago Indian Society," *Social Forces* 36:251–256.

———, 1960, "A Survey of Native Peoples of North Borneo," *Sociologus* 10:170–174.

———, 1961a, "Ethnohistorical Relationships and Patterns of Customary Behavior among North Borneo Native Peoples," *Sociologus* 11:51–63.

———, 1961b, "A Tambunan Dusun Origin Myth," *Journal of American Folklore* 74: 68–78.

———, 1962a, "Form, Function and Culture History of a Borneo Musical Instrument," *Oceania* 32:178–185.

———, 1962b, "Tambunan Dusun Social Structure," *Sociologus* 12:141–158.

———, 1962c, "Archaeological Research in North Borneo," *Asian Perspectives: The Bulletin of the Far Eastern Prehistory Association* 6:230–231.

———, 1963a, "The Form and Functions of Tambunan Dusun Riddles," *Journal of American Folklore* 76:95–110; 141–181.

———, 1963b, "The Form of a North Borneo Nativistic Behavior," *American Anthropologist* 65:543–551.

———, 1965, *The Dusun; A North Borneo Society.* New York: Holt, Rinehart and Winston, Inc.

———, 1966, "Cultural Structuring of Tactile Experiences in a Borneo Society," *American Anthropologist* 68:27–39.

———, 1967, *Field Methods in the Study of Culture.* New York: Holt, Rinehart and Winston, Inc.

———, 1968, "Ethnographic Research in Northern Borneo," *Oceania,* 39:70–80.

WOLFENSTEIN, M., 1955, "French Parents Take Their Children to the Park," in *Childhood in Contemporary Cultures,* M. Mead and M. Wolfenstein, eds. Chicago: University of Chicago Press, pp. 106–107.

WOOD, D. P. J., 1957, "The Amiable Rice-growers of North Borneo," *Geographical Magazine* 30:13–22.

———, and B. J. MOSER, 1958, "Village Communities in the Tambunan Area of British North Borneo." *Geographical Journal* 124:56–68.

WOOLLEY, G. C., 1932a, *Dusun Custom in the Putatan District,* compiled by Pangeran Osman bin O.K.K. Pangeran Haji Omar, Deputy Assistant District Officer, Putatan; translated by G. C. Woolley, North Borneo Civil Service. Sandakan: Government Printing Office (reprinted in English in 1962 as *Dusun Custom in Putatan District.* Native Affairs Bulletin No. 7. Jesselton: North Borneo Government Printing Office.

———, 1932b, *Kwijau Adat: Customs Regulating Inheritance Amongst the Kwijau Tribe of the Interior,* Native Affairs Bulletin No. 6. Sandakan: Government Printing Office.

———, 1932c, *Dusun Adat: Some Customs of the Dusuns of Tambunan and Ranau, West Coast Residency, North Borneo.* Sandakan: Government Printing Office (reprinted in Malay, 1962, as *Adat Dusun: Adat² Dusun di-Tambunan dan Ranau,* Native Affairs Bulletin No. 5. Jesselton: North Borneo Government Printing Office).

———, 1936a, *Dusun Adat: Customs Regulating Inheritance Amongst the Dusun Tribes in the Coastal Plains of Putatan and Papar.* Sandakan: Government Printing Office (reprinted in Malay, in 1953, as *Adat Dusun: istiadat yang di-pesakai turun menurun di-masharakat Suku² Dusun yang di-pantai tanah rata Papar dan Putatan.* Native Affairs Bulletin No. 4. Jesselton: North Borneo Government Printing Office.

———, 1936b, *Tuaran Adat: Some Customs of the Dusuns of Tuaran, West Coast Residency, North Borneo.* Native Affairs Bulletin No. 2. Sandakan: Government Printing Office.

Recommended reading

Summary of Societies

Abipón	Hopi	Paiute
Ainu	Ifaluk	Palaung
Alor	Ifugao	Papago
American	Ilocos	Puerto Ricans
Andamanese	Israelis	Pukapukans
Arab	Japanese	Pygmies
Arapesh	Javanese	Rājpūts
Arunta (Aranda)	Jicarilla[2]	Riffians
Ashanti	Kaingang	Russians
Azande	Kiwai	R'wala
Baiga	Kutenai	Samoans
Bali	Kwakiutl	Sanpoil
Basuto	Kwoma	Siriono
Bemba	Lakher	Slave
Bena	Lamba	Tallensi
Bushman	Lapp	Tanala
Chaga (Tschagga)	Lepcha	Taos
Chamorro	Malekula	Teton
Cheyenne	Manus	Thonga
Chinese	Maori	Tikopia
Chiricahua[2]	Marquesans	Trobriands
Dahomeans	Masai	Venda
Deoli[3]	Mexican	Wapishana
Dobuans	Murngin	Warrau
English	Navaho	Witoto
Eskimo	Ngoni	Wogeo
Fijians	Nuer	Yagua
French	Nyakyusa	Yakut
Flathead	Okinawa	Yungar
German	Omaha	Zadruga[4]
Gusii	Otong-Javanese	Zuni

---

[1] The selected references given here are not intended to be exhaustive nor to comprise an "up to date" bibliography for each society. Rather, these references are readings which, in my judgment, represent the descriptions of enculturation which can be used by students in comparative studies.

[2] The Chiricahua and Jicarilla both are "Apache" groups. The Chiricahua aboriginal range was in southeastern Arizona and along the southwestern New Mexico border with Arizona. The Jicarilla aboriginal range was in north and eastern New Mexico along the borders of Colorado, Oklahoma and Texas. The Chiricahua are "Western Apache."

[3] "Deoli" is a pseudonym for a community of high caste Hindus in the Indian state of Rajasthan.

[4] The term "Zadruga" refers to a peasant cooperative association in South Slav culture and not to a specific society. See E. R. Wolf, 1966, *Peasants,* Englewood Cliffs, N.J., Prentice-Hall, pp. 38–66.

Abipón (South America–Argentina)

DOBRIZHOFFER, M., 1822, *An Account of the Abipónes, An Equestrian People of Paraguay*. London: Murray.

Ainu (Japan)

BATCHELOR, J., n.d., *The Ainu of Japan*. New York: Revell.

———, 1901, *The Ainu and their Folk-lore*. London: The Religious Tract Society.

———, 1927, *Ainu Life and Lore*. Tokyo: Kyobunkwan.

Alor (Indonesia)

DUBOIS, CORA, 1944, *The People of Alor: A Socio-Psychological Study of an East Indian Island*. Minneapolis: University of Minnesota Press.

Americans (U.S.)

BARKER, R. G. and H. F. WRIGHT, 1955, *The Midwest and Its Children*. New York: Harper & Row.

FISCHER, J. L. and A. FISCHER, 1966, *The New Englanders of Orchard Town, U.S.A.*, in Six Cultures Series, Vol. 5, B. Whiting, ed. New York: Wiley.

GORER, GEOFFREY, 1948, *The American People*. New York: Norton.

KLUCKHOHN, C. and F. KLUCKHOHN, 1947, "American Culture: Generalized Orientations and Class Patterns," in *Conflicts of Power in Modern Culture: Seventh Symposium*, Lyman Bryson, ed. New York: Conference on Science, Philosophy and Religion pp. 106–128.

HAVINGHURST, R. J., P. BOWMAN, G. LIDDLE, C. MATTHEWS, and G. PIERCE, 1962, *Growing Up in River City*. New York: Wiley.

LANTIS, MARGARET (special editor), 1955, "The U.S.A. as Anthropologists See It," *American Anthropologist* 57:1113–1295.

MCCLELLAND, DAVID, 1961, *The Achieving Society*. Princeton, N.J.: Van Nostrand.

MEAD, MARGARET, 1942, *And Keep Your Powder Dry: An Anthropologist Looks at America*. New York: Morrow.

———, 1948, "The Contemporary American Family as an Anthropologist See It," *American Journal of Sociology* 53:453–459.

RIESMAN, DAVID, 1950, *The Lonely Crowd*. New Haven, Conn.: Yale University Press.

———, 1952, *Faces in the Crowd*. New Haven, Conn.: Yale University Press.

SEARS, R. R., E. E. MACCOBY, and H. LEVIN, 1957, *Patterns of Child Rearing*. New York: Harper & Row.

WARNER, W. LLOYD and P. S. LUNT, 1941, *The Social Life of a Modern Community*. New Haven, Conn.: Yale University Press.

WEST, JAMES, 1945, *Plainville, U.S.A.* New York: Columbia University Press (see also A. Gallaher, 1961, *Plainville Fifteen Years Later*. New York: Columbia University Press).

WOLFENSTEIN, M., 1957, *Disaster: A Psychological Essay*. New York: Free Press.

Andamanese (Andaman Islands)

MAN, E. H., 1883, *On the Aboriginal Inhabitants of the Andaman Islands*. London: Royal Anthropological Institute of Great Britain and Ireland.

RADCLIFFE-BROWN, A. R., 1933, *The Andaman Islanders*. New York: Cambridge.

Arab (Egypt)

AMMAR, H., 1954 (1966), *Growing Up in an Egyptian Village*. London: Routledge.

Arab (Palestinian Arabs)

GRANQVIST, H., 1931, *Marriage Conditions in a Palestinian Village*. 2 vols. Helsingfors: Akademiche buchhandlung (reprinted in 1935).

———, 1947, *Birth and Childhood among the Arabs: Studies in a Muhammadan Village in Palestine*. Helsingfors: Söderström.

———, 1950, *Child Problems among the Arabs*. Helsingfors: Söderström.

Arapesh (New Guinea)

MEAD, MARGARET, 1935, "The Mountain Dwelling Arapesh," in *Sex and Temperament in Three Primitive Societies*. New York: Morrow (reprinted 1950, New York: Mentor Books, M56).

———, 1937, "The Arapesh of New Guinea," in *Cooperation and Competition among Primitive Peoples*. New York: McGraw-Hill. (Rev. ed. 1961. Boston: Beacon.)

———, 1938–1939, *The Mountain Arapesh*, Anthropological Papers of the American Museum of Natural History 36:145–349; 37:317–451; 40:163–419; 41:289–390.

Arunta (Australia)

SPENCER, BALDWIN and F. J. GILLEN, 1899, *Native Tribes of Central Australia*. London: Macmillan.

———, 1928, *The Arunta*. 2 vols. London: Macmillan.

Ashanti (Africa–Ghana)

RATTRAY, R. S., 1929, *Ashanti Law and Constitution*. London: Oxford.

———, 1959, *Religion and Art in Ashanti*. London: Oxford.

Azande (Africa–Democratic Republic of Congo)

EVANS-PRITCHARD, E. E., 1937, *Witchcraft, Oracles, and Magic among the Azande*. Oxford: Clarendon Press.

Baiga (India)

ELWIN, V., 1939, *The Baiga*. London: J. Murray.

Bali (Indonesia)

BATESON, G., 1949, "Bali: The Value System of a Steady State," in *Social Structure: Essays Presented to A. R. Radcliffe-Brown*, M. Fortes, ed. Oxford: Clarendon Press.

BATESON, G. and M. MEAD, 1942, *Balinese Character: A Photographic Analysis*, W. G. Valentine, ed., Vol. 2. New York: Special Publication of the New York Academy of Sciences (reprinted in 1962).

BELO, JANE, 1935, "The Balinese Temper," *Character and Personality* 4:120–146.

———, 1936, "A Study of a Balinese Family," *American Anthropologist* 38:12–31.

———, 1960, *Trance in Bali*. New York: Columbia University Press.

MEAD, MARGARET, 1949, *Male and Female: A Study of the Sexes in a Changing World*. New York: Morrow (reprinted 1955, Mentor Books, MD150).

———, 1951, "Research on Primitive Children," in *Manual of Child Psychology*, Leonard Carmichael, ed. New York: Wiley, pp. 735–780.

———, and FRANCES G. MACGREGOR, 1951, *Growth and Culture: A Photographic Study of Balinese Childhood*. New York: Putnam.

Basuto (Africa–South Africa)

ASHTON, HUGO, 1952, *The Basuto*. London: Oxford University Press.

Bemba (Africa–Zambia)

RICHARDS, A. I., 1956, *Chisungu*. New York: Grove.

Bena (Africa–Tanzania)

CULWICK, A. T. and G. M. CULWICK, 1935, *Ubena of the River*. London: Allen.

Bushman (Africa–South Africa)

THOMAS, ELIZABETH MARSHALL, 1959, *The Harmless People*. New York: Knopf.

VAN DER POST, L., 1958, *The Lost World of the Kalahari*. New York: Morrow.

———, 1961, *The Heart of the Hunter*. New York: Morrow.

Chaga (Africa–Tanzania)

DUNDAS, C., 1924, *Kilimanjaro and Its People*. London: Witherby.

RAUM, O. F., 1940, *Chaga Childhood*. London: Oxford University Press.

Chamorro (Micronesia–Guam)

THOMPSON, L., 1947, *Guam and Its People*. Princeton, N.J.: Princeton University Press.

Cheyenne (U.S.)

GRINNELL, GEORGE B., 1915, *The Fighting Cheyennes*. New York: Scribner.

———, 1925, *The Cheyenne Indians: Their History and Ways of Life*. 2 vols. New Haven, Conn.: Yale University Press.

HOEBEL, E. A., 1960, *The Cheyennes: Indians of the Great Plains*. New York: Holt, Rinehart and Winston, Inc.

LLEWELLYN, K. N. and E. A. HOEBEL, 1941, *The Cheyenne Way: Conflict and Case Law in Primitive Jurisprudence*. Norman, Oklahoma: University of Oklahoma Press.

Chinese (Mainland)

BUNZEL, RUTH, 1950, *Explorations in Chinese Character.* New York: Columbia University Research in Contemporary Cultures (dittoed).

CHIANG YEE, 1952, *A Chinese Childhood.* New York: John Day.

FENG HAN-CHI, 1948, *The Chinese Kinship System.* Cambridge, Mass.: Harvard University Press.

FRIED, M., 1953, *The Fabric of Chinese Society.* New York: Praeger.

HSU, F. L. K., 1955, *Americans and Chinese: Two Ways of Life.* London: Cresset.

HU HSIEN CHIN, 1948, *The Common Descent Group in China and Its Functions,* Viking Fund Publications in Anthropology, No. 10. New York: Viking Fund.

YANG, M. C., 1945, *A Chinese Village.* New York: Columbia University Press.

Chiricahua (U.S.)

OPLER, M. E., 1941, *An Apache Life Way.* Chicago: University of Chicago Press.

Dahomeans (Africa–Dahomey)

HERSKOVITS, M. J., 1938, *Dahomey: An Ancient West African Kingdom.* New York: Augustin.

"Deoli" (India–Rajasthan)

CARSTAIRS, G. M., 1958, *The Twice Born: A Study of a Community of High Caste Hindus.* Bloomington: Indiana University Press.

Dobuans (Melanesia–D'Entrecasteaux Islands)

FORTUNE, R. B., 1932, *Sorcerers of Dobu.* New York: Dutton.

English (U.K.)

GORER, G., 1955, *Exploring English Character.* New York: Criterion.

SODDY, K. ed., 1956, *Mental Health and Infant Development.* 2 vols. New York: Basic Books (see Vol. 1, pp. 54–86, Vol. 2 *passim*).

YOUNG, M. D. and P. WILLMOTT, 1957, *Family and Kinship in East London.* London: Routledge.

Eskimo (Alaska, Northern Canada, Greenland)

JENNESS, D., 1922, *The Life of the Copper Eskimo,* Report of the Canadian Arctic Expedetion, 1913–1918. Ottawa: Acland.

LANTIS, M., 1960, *Eskimo Childhood and Interpersonal Relationships.* Seattle: University of Washington Press.

MIRSKY, JEANNETTE, 1937, "The Eskimos of Greenland," in *Cooperation and Competition among Primitive Peoples,* Margaret Mead, ed., New York: McGraw-Hill, pp. 51–86 (rev. ed. 1961, Boston: Beacon).

Fijians (Polynesia–Fiji)

QUAIN, B., 1948, *Fijian Village.* Chicago: University of Chicago Press.

French (France)

BERNOT, LUCIEN and RENE BLANCHARD, 1953, *Nouville, un Village Français,* Travaux et Memoires de l'Institut d'Ethnologie, No. 57. Paris: Institut d'Ethnologie.

METRAUX, RHODA and M. MEAD, 1954, *Themes in French Culture: A Preface to a Study of a French Community.* Stanford: Stanford University Press.

SODDY, K. ed., 1956, *Mental Health and Infant Development.* 2 vols. New York: Basic Books (see Vol. 1, pp. 15–53, Vol. 2 *passim*).

WYLIE, L. W., 1957, *Village in the Vancluse.* Cambridge, Mass.: Harvard University Press.

Flathead (U.S.)

TURNEY-HIGH, H., 1937, *The Flathead Indians of Montana,* Memoirs of the American Anthropological Association, No. 47. Menasha, Wisconsin: American Anthropological Association.

German (Germany)

BATESON, GREGORY, 1943, "Cultural and Thematic Analysis of Fictional Films," *Transaction,* New York Academy of Sciences, Series 2, 5:72–78.

DICKS, H. V., 1950, "Personality Traits and National Socialist Ideology," *Human Relations* 3:111–154.

ERIKSON, E. H., 1950, *Childhood and Society*. New York: Norton.

FROMM, E., 1941, *Escape from Freedom*. New York: Holt, Rinehart and Winston, Inc.

LOWIE, ROBERT, 1945, *The German People: A Social Portrait to 1914*. New York: Holt, Rinehart and Winston, Inc.

METRAUX, RHODA, 1955, "A Portrait of the Family in German Juvenile Fiction," in *Childhood in Contemporary Cultures*, Margaret Mead and Martha Wolfenstein, eds. Chicago: University of Chicago Press, pp. 253–276.

RODNICK, DAVID, 1948, *Postwar Germans: An Anthropologist's Account*. New Haven, Conn.: Yale University Press.

Gusii (Africa–Kenya)

LEVINE, R. and B. LEVINE, 1955, *Nyansongo: A Gusii Community in Kenya*, in Six Cultures Series, Vol. 2, B. Whiting, ed. New York: Wiley.

Hopi (U.S.)

DENNIS, WAYNE, 1940, *The Hopi Child*. New York: Appleton.

SIMMONS, L. W., 1942, *Sun Chief: The Autobiography of a Hopi Indian*. New Haven, Conn.: Yale University Press.

Ifaluk (Micronesia–Caroline Islands)

BURROWS, E. and M. E. SPIRO, 1953, *An Atoll Culture: Ethnography of Ifaluk in the Central Carolines*. New Haven, Conn.: Human Relations Area Files.

Ifugao (Philippines)

BARTON, R. F., 1930, *The Half-Way Sun*. New York: Brewer and Warren.

———, 1938, *Philippine Pagans: The Autobiographies of Three Ifugaos*. London: Routledge.

Ilocos (Philippines)

NYDEGGER, W. F. and C. NYDEGGER, 1966, *Tarong: An Ilocos Barrio in the Philippines*, in Six Cultures Series, Vol. 6, B. Whiting, ed. New York: Wiley.

Israelis (Middle East–Israel)

SPIRO, M. E., 1956, *Kibbutz: Venture into Utopia*. Cambridge, Mass.: Harvard University Press.

———, 1958, *Children of the Kibbutz*. Cambridge, Mass.: Harvard University Press.

RABIN, A. I., 1965, *Growing Up in the Kibbutz*. New York: Springer.

Japanese (Japan)

BEARDSLEY, R. K., 1951, "The Household in the Status System of Japanese Villages," Occasional Papers, No. 1, University of Michigan Center for Japanese Studies. Ann Arbor: University of Michigan Press.

BENEDICT, RUTH, 1946, *The Chrysanthemum and the Sword*. Boston: Houghton Mifflin.

DORE, R. P., 1958, *City Life in Japan: A Study of a Tokyo Ward*. Berkeley: University of California Press.

SILBERMAN, B. S., 1962, *Japanese Character and Culture: A Book of Selected Readings*. Tucson: University of Arizona Press.

Javanese (Indonesia)

GEERTZ, H., 1961, *The Javanese Family: A Study of Kinship and Socialization*. New York: Free Press.

Jicarilla (U.S.)

OPLER, M. E., 1946, *Childhood and Youth in Jicarilla Apache Society*. Los Angeles: The Southwest Museum.

Kaingang (South America–Brazil)

HENRY, JULES, 1936, "The Personality of the Kaingang Indians," *Character and Personality* 5:113–123.

———, 1941, *Jungle People: The Kaingang Tribe of the Highlands of Brazil*. New York: J. J. Augustin.

Kiwai (New Guinea)

LANDTMAN, G., 1927, *The Kiwai Papuans of British New Guinea*. London: Macmillan.

Kutenai (Canada)

TURNEY-HIGH, H. H., 1941, *Ethnography of the Kutenai*, Memoirs of the American Anthropological Association, No. 36, Menasha, Wisconsin: American Anthropological Association.

Kwakiutl (Canada)

BOAS, FRANZ, 1921, *Ethnology of the Kwakiutl,* in U.S. Bureau of American Ethnology, Washington, D. C., No. 35, parts 1–2, pp. 41–1481. See also, H. Codere, ed., 1966, *Kwakiutl Ethnography,* Chicago: University of Chicago Press.

———, 1932, "Current Beliefs of the Kwakiutl Indians," *Journal of American Folklore* No. 176, 45:177–260.

FORD, C. S., 1941, *Smoke from their Fires: The Life of the Kwakiutl Chief.* New Haven, Conn.: Yale University Press.

WALCOTT, H. F., 1967, *A Kwakiutl Village and School.* New York: Holt, Rinehart and Winston, Inc.

Kwoma (New Guinea)

WHITING, J. W. M., 1941, *Becoming a Kwoma.* New Haven, Conn.: Yale University Press.

Lakher (India)

PARRY, N. E., 1932, *The Lakhers.* London: Macmillan.

Lamba (Africa–Zambia)

DOKE, C. M., 1931, *The Lambas of Northern Rhodesia.* London: Harrap & Co.

Lapp (Finland/Russia/Sweden/Norway)

SHEFFER, J., 1704, *The History of Lappland.* London.

TURI, J., 1931, *Turi's Book of Lappland.* London: Harper.

Lepcha (Nepal)

GORER, G., 1938, *Himalayan Village.* London: Michael Joseph.

MORRIS, J., 1938, *Living with Lepchas.* London: Heinemann.

Malekula (Melanesia–New Hebrides)

DEACON, A. B., 1934, *Malekula.* London: Routledge.

LEGGATT, T. W., 1893, *Malekula, New Hebrides,* Reports of the Australian Association for the Advancement of Science, No. 4, pp. 697–708.

Manus (Melanesia–Admirality Islands)

FORTUNE, R. F., 1935, *Manus Religion.* Philadelphia: American Philosophical Society.

MEAD, MARGARET, 1930, *Growing Up in New Guinea.* New York: Morrow.

———, 1932, "An Investigation of the Thought of Primitive Children, with Special Reference to Animism," *Journal of the Royal Anthropological Institute* 62:173–190.

———, 1949, *Male and Female.* New York: Morrow.

———, 1956, *New Lives for Old: Cultural Transformation—Manus, 1928–1956.* New York: Morrow.

Maori (Polynesia–New Zealand)

AUSUBEL, D. P., 1961, *Maori Youth,* Publication in Psychology No. 11. Victoria: University of Wellington, Wellington, N.Z.

BEST, E., 1924, *The Maori,* Polynesian Society Memoir, No. 5. 2 vols. Wellington, N.Z.: Polynesian Society.

BUCK, P. H., 1950, *The Coming of the Maori.* Wellington, N.Z.: Maori Purposes Fund Board.

RITCHIE, J. E., 1963, *The Making of a Maori.* Wellington: A. H. Reed and A. W. Reed.

Marquesans (Polynesia–Marquesas Islands)

HANDY, E. S. C., 1923, *The Native Culture in the Marquesas,* Bernice P. Bishop Museum Bulletin No. 9. Honolulu, Hawaii: Bernice P. Bishop Museum.

LINTON, R., 1939, "Marquesan Culture," in *The Individual and His Society,* A. Kardiner, ed. New York: Columbia University Press, pp. 137–196.

Masai (Africa–Kenya)

HOLLIS, A. C., 1905, *The Masai: Their Language and Folklore.* Oxford: Clarendon Press.

MERKER, M., 1904, *Die Masai.* Berlin: Reimer.

Mexican (Mexico)

LEWIS, O., 1951, *Life in a Mexican Village: Tepoztlan Restudied.* Urbana: University of Illinois Press.

———, 1959, *Five Families: Mexican Case Studies in the Culture of Poverty*. New York: Basic Books.

———, 1961, *The Children of Sanchez: Autobiography of a Mexican Family*. New York: Random House, Inc.

REDFIELD, ROBERT, 1930, *Tepoztlan: A Mexican Village*. Chicago: University of Chicago Press.

ROMNEY, K. and R. ROMNEY, 1966, *The Mixtecans of Juxtalhuaca, Mexico*, in Six Cultures Series, Vol. 4, B. Whiting, ed. New York: Wiley.

Murngin (Australia)

WARNER, W. L., 1937, *A Black Civilization*. New York: Harper & Row.

Navaho (U.S.)

KLUCKHOHN, CLYDE, 1947, "Some Aspects of Navaho Infancy and Early Childhood," in *Psychoanalysis and the Social Sciences*, G. Roheim, ed. Vol. 1, New York: International Universities Press, pp. 37–86.

———, 1960, "A Navaho Politician," in *In the Company of Man*, J. B. Casagrande, ed. New York: Harper & Row, pp. 439–465.

——— and D. LEIGHTON, 1946, *The Navaho*. Cambridge, Mass.: Harvard University Press.

KLUCKHOHN, FLORENCE and F. L. STRODTBECK, 1961, *Variations in Value Orientations*. New York: Harper & Row.

LEIGHTON, D. and C. KLUCKHOHN, 1947, *Children of the People*. Cambridge, Mass.: Harvard University Press.

Ngoni (Africa–Malawi)

READ, MARGARET, 1956, *The Ngoni of Nyasaland*. New York: Oxford University Press.

———, 1960, *Children of their Fathers: Growing Up among the Ngoni of Nyasaland*. New Haven, Conn.: Yale University Press.

———, 1968, *Growing Up among the Ngoni of Malawi*. New York: Holt, Rinehart and Winston, Inc.

Nuer (Africa–Sudan)

EVANS-PRITCHARD, E. E., 1940, *The Nuer: A Description of the Modes of Livelihood and Political Institutions of a Nilotic People*. Oxford: Oxford University Press.

Nyakyusa (Africa–Tanzania)

WILSON, M., 1951, *Good Company*. London: Oxford University Press.

Okinawa (Ryukyu Islands–Pacific)

MARETZKI, T. and H. MARETZKI, 1966, *Taira: An Okinawa Village*, in Six Cultures Series, Vol. 7, B. Whiting, ed. New York: Wiley.

Omaha (U.S.)

FLETCHER, A. C. and F. LaFLESCHE, 1911, *The Omaha Tribe*, Annual Reports of the Bureau of American Ethnology, No. 27, pp. 15–672.

FORTUNE, R. F., 1932, *Omaha Secret Societies*. New York: Columbia University Press.

Ontong-Javanese (Melanesia–Solomon Islands)

HOGBIN, H. I., 1930, "Spirits and the Healing of the Sick in Ontong Java," *Oceania* 1:146–166.

———, 1931, "Education at Ontong Java," *American Anthropologist* 33:601–614.

Paiute (U.S.)

WHITING, B. B., 1950, *Paiute Sorcery*. New York: Viking Fund Publications in Anthropology, No. 15.

Palaung (Burma)

MILNE, L., 1924, *The Home of an Eastern Clan*. Oxford: Clarendon Press.

Papago (U.S.)

JOSEPH, A., R. B. SPICER, and J. CHESKY, 1949, *The Desert People*. Chicago: University of Chicago Press.

UNDERHILL, R., 1939, *Social Organization of the Papago Indians*, Columbia University Contributions to Anthropology, No. 30. New York: Columbia University Press.

WILLIAMS, T. R., 1958, "The Structure of the Socialization Process in Papago Indian Society," *Social Forces* 36:251–256.

Puerto Ricans (Puerto Rico)
LANDY, DAVID, 1959, *Tropical Childhood: Cultural Transmission and Learning in a Rural Puerto Rican Village.* Chapel Hill: University of North Carolina Press.
Pukapukans (Polynesia–Danger Island)
BEAGLEHOLE, E. and P. BEAGLEHOLE, 1938, *Ethnology of Pukapuka,* Bernice P. Bishop Museum Bulletin No. 150. Honolulu, Hawaii: Bernice P. Bishop Museum.
———, 1941, "Personality Development in Pukapukan Children," in *Language, Culture and Personality,* L. Spier, A. I. Hallowell and S. S. Newman, eds. Menasha, Wisconsin: Sapir Memorial Fund, pp. 282–288.
Pygmies (Africa–Democratic Republic of the Congo)
TURNBULL, COLIN, 1962, *The Lonely African.* New York: Simon and Schuster.
Rājpūts (India)
MINTURN, L. and J. T. HITCHCOCK, 1966, *The Rajpūts of Khalapur, India,* in Six Cultures Series, Vol. 3, B. Whiting, ed. New York: Wiley.
Riffians (Africa–Morocco)
COON, C. S., 1931, *Tribes of the Rif.* Harvard African Studies, Vol. 9. Cambridge, Mass.: Peabody Museum of Harvard University.
Russians (U.S.S.R.)
BAUER, RAYMOND et al., 1961, *How the Soviet System Works: Cultural, Psychological and Social Themes.* New York: Vintage Books.
GORER, G. and J. RICKMAN, 1950, *The People of Great Russia.* New York: Chanticlear Press.
MEAD, MARGARET, 1951, *Soviet Attitudes toward Authority.* New York: Morrow.
———, 1951, "What Makes Soviet Character?" *Natural History* 60:296–303.
———, 1954, "The Swaddling Hypothesis: Its Reception," *American Anthropologist* 56: 395–409.
MILLER, W., 1960, *The Russians as People.* New York: Dutton.
R'wala (Middle East–Syria, Iraq)
MUSIL, A., 1928, *The Manners and Customs of the Rwala Bedouins.* New York: Czech Academy of Sciences and Arts and Charles R. Crane.
Samoans (Polynesia–Samoa)
HIROA, TE RANGI (P. H. BUCK), 1930, *Samoan Material Culture,* Bernice P. Bishop Museum Bulletin No. 75. Honolulu, Hawaii: Bernice P. Bishop Museum.
MEAD, MARGARET, 1928, *Coming of Age in Samoa.* New York: Morrow (reprinted New York: Morrow, 1961, Apollo Editions A-30).
———, 1928, "A Lapse of Animism among a Primitive People," *Psyche,* 9:72–77.
———, 1928, "The Role of the Individual in Samoan Culture," *Journal of the Royal Anthropological Institute,* 58:481–495.
———, 1930, *Social Organization of Manua,* Bernice P. Bishop Museum Bulletin No. 76. Honolulu, Hawaii: Bernice P. Bishop Museum.
SU'APA'IA, KIPENI, 1962, *Samoa: The Polynesian Paradise.* New York: Exposition Press.
Sanpoil (U.S.)
RAY, V. F., 1933, *The Sanpoil and Nespelem.* Seattle: University of Washington Press.
Siriono (South America–Bolivia)
HOLMBERG, A. R., 1950, *Nomads of the Long Bow,* Institute of Social Anthropology, Smithsonian Institution, Publication No. 10. Washington, D. C.: U. S. Government Printing Office.
Slave (Canada)
HONIGMANN, J. J., 1946, *Ethnography and Acculturation of the Fort Nelson Slave,* Yale University Publications in Anthropology, No. 33. New Haven, Conn.: Yale University Press.
Tallensi (Africa–Ghana)
FORTES, M., 1938, *Social and Psychological Aspects of Education in Taleland.* London: Oxford University Press.

Tanala (Malagasy Republic)

LINTON, R., 1933, *The Tanala,* Publications of the Field Museum of Natural History, Anthropological Series, Vol. 22. Chicago: Field Museum of Natural History.

——, 1939, "The Tanala of Madagascar," in *The Individual and His Society,* A. Kardiner, ed. New York: Columbia University Press, pp. 251–290.

Taos (U.S.)

PARSONS, E., 1936, *Taos Pueblo,* General Series in Anthropology, No. 2. Menasha, Wis.: Banta.

Teton (U.S.)

ERIKSON, E., 1939, "Observations on Sioux Education," *Journal of Psychology* 7:101–156.

MACGREGOR, G., 1946, *Warriors without Weapons.* Chicago: University of Chicago Press.

Thonga (Africa–Mozambique)

JUNOD, H. A., 1962, *The Life of a South African Tribe.* New Hyde Park, N. Y.: University Books.

Tikopia (Melanesia–Santa Cruz Islands)

FIRTH, R., 1936, *We, The Tikopia.* New York: American Book.

Trobriands (Melanesia–Trobriand Islands)

LEE, D., 1940, "Primitive System of Values," *Philosophy of Science* 7:355–378.

MALINOWSKI, B., 1926, *Crime and Custom in Savage Society.* London: Routledge.

——, 1927, *Sex and Repression in Savage Society.* London: Routledge.

——, 1929, *The Sexual Life of Savages in North-West Melanesia: An Ethnographic Account of Courtship, Marriage and Family Life Among the Natives of the Trobriand Islands, British New Guinea.* 2 vols. New York: Liveright.

——, 1932, *Argonauts of the Western Pacific.* London: Routledge.

——, 1935, *Coral Gardens and their Magic: A Study of the Method of Tilling of the Soil and of Agricultural Rites in the Trobriand Islands.* 2 vols. New York: American Books.

Venda (Africa–South Africa)

STAYT, H. A., 1931, *The BaVenda.* London: Oxford University Press.

Wapishana (South America–Guyana/Surinam)

FARABEE, W. C., 1918, *The Central Arawaks.* Anthropological Publication of the University of Pennsylvania Museum, No. 9. Philadelphia: University of Pennsylvania Press, pp. 13–131.

Warrau (South America–Venezuela–Guyana)

SCHOMBURGK, R., 1922, *Travels in British Guinea, 1840–44,* Vol. 1. Georgetown, British Guinea: Daily Chronicle Office.

Witoto (South America–Columbia)

WHIFFEN, T., 1915, *The North-West Amazons.* New York: Duffield.

Wogeo (New Guinea)

HOGBIN, H. I., 1943, "A New Guinea Infancy: From Conception to Weaning in Wogeo," *Oceania* 13:285–309.

——, 1946, "A New Guinea Childhood: From Weaning till the Eighth Year in Wogeo," *Oceania* 16:275–296.

Yagua (South America–Peru)

FEJOS, P., 1943, *Ethnography of the Yagua,* Viking Fund Publications in Anthropology, No. 1. New York: The Wenner-Grenn Foundation.

Yakut (U.S.S.R.–Northern Siberia)

IOKHEL'SON, V. I., 1933, *The Yakut,* Anthropological Papers of the American Museum of Natural History, No. 33, pp. 33–225.

Yungar (Australia)

GREY, G., 1841, *Journals of Two Expeditions of Discovery in Northwest and Western Australia.* London: Boone.

Zadruga (Eastern Europe)

TOMASIC, DINKO, 1948, *Personality and Culture in Eastern European Politics.* New York: G. W. Stewart.

Zuni (U.S.)

BENEDICT, RUTH, 1934, "The Pueblos of New Mexico," in *Patterns of Culture*. Boston and New York: Houghton Mifflin, pp. 57–129.

——, 1935, *Zuni Mythology*. Columbia University Contributions to Anthropology, No. 21. 2 vols. New York: Columbia University Press.

BUNZEL, RUTH, 1929, *The Pueblo Potter: A Study of the Creative Imagination in Primitive Art*. New York: Columbia University Press.

——, 1933, *Zuni Texts*, Publications of the American Ethnological Society, No. 15. New York: G. E. Stechert and Co.

PARSONS, E. G., 1917, *Notes on Zuni, Part I*. Memoirs of the American Anthropological Association, Vol. 4, No. 3, pp. 151–225.

——, 1917, *Notes on Zuni, Part II*. Memoirs of the American Anthropological Association, Vol. 4, No. 4, pp. 227–338.

Linguistic chart

	Front	Front Rounded	Central	Back Rounded
High	i	ü	ɨ I	u
Mid	e		ė E	o
Mid-low	əe			
Low	a		à A	ɑ A

* ALEVOLAR, VOICED, VIBRANT *r*.
  ALVEOLAR, VOICED, VIBRANT, TRILLED *r*.
  DIPHTHONGS: eu, au, ai, ua, ia, io, uo, iu, oi, ie, iė, ei, eė, ea, eà, ao, àe, àa, àu, oe, ou, ui, uà.
* After B. Bloch and G. L. Trager, 1942, *Outline of Linguistic Analysis,* Baltimore, E. Waverly Press, Inc., p. 22, "Classification of Vowels."

	Bilabial	Labio-dental	Alveolar	Velar	Glottal
Voiceless STOPS	p		t	k	ʾ
Voiced	b		d	g	
Voiceless FRICATIVES			s	x	
Voiced		v			h
Nasal, Voiced FRICTIONLESS	m		n	ŋ N	
Lateral, Voiced			ɫ		

* After K. L. Pike, 1947, *Phonemics: A Technique for Reducing Languages to Writing,* Ann Arbor, University of Michigan Press, Chart 2, p. 7, "Symbols for Non-syllabic Nonvocoids with Egressive Lung Air."
  The capital letters (I, E, A, *A,* N) have been used in some other publications (see Williams 1963a, 1965) due to the expense of casting type for the special linguistic symbols commonly used by anthropologists. In reading these particular publications the substitution of the symbols noted above for the capital letters can be followed easily by reference to the lower-right-hand corner of the appropriate category on this chart.

31